AF255220

Lessons from the Elk Woods

Lessons from the Elk Woods

Hunter's Devotional

BRAD SCHWIN

Foreword by Corey Jacobsen

RESOURCE *Publications* · Eugene, Oregon

LESSONS FROM THE ELK WOODS
Hunter's Devotional

Resource Publications
An Imprint of Wipf and Stock Publishers
199 W. 8th Ave., Suite 3
Eugene, OR 97401

www.wipfandstock.com

PAPERBACK ISBN: 978-1-6667-7866-3
HARDCOVER ISBN: 978-1-6667-7867-0
EBOOK ISBN: 978-1-6667-7868-7

06/14/23

This devotional book is dedicated to:

My wife, Michele, who without her unfailing love and support, would have never made this project possible;

My three sons, Caleb, Kyle, and Lucas, who has given this dad more joy in fatherhood than any man deserves;

My parents, Vern and Sharon, who instilled in me at an early age, a love for hunting and the outdoors;

My brother and hunting partner Doug, who inspires and challenges me in both my outdoor pursuits and my faith;

My close hunting buddies, who have helped make each trip to elk camp a lasting memory;

And most importantly, to my Lord and Savior Jesus Christ, who continually reveals Himself to me in new ways, each time I step into the elk woods.

Contents

Foreword by Corey Jacobsen | ix

Price of Admission | 1

J-Scouting | 4

Have To or Get To | 6

Read The Signs | 8

Failure Is an Option | 10

When in Doubt Walk it Out | 13

No Plan B | 15

Two Better Than One | 17

Game Trails | 19

Get Your Sights Right | 21

Bugle Fest Interloper | 24

No Day Wasted | 27

Attitude Adjustment | 29

Tell Me Your Stories, Boys | 31

Boots on the Ground | 34

Blood Trail | 37

F.O.O.L. | 40

Shangri-la | 43

The Treacherous Path | 45

When the Forest is Silent | 48

Speak Life | 50

Fear Factor | 53

Soul Recharge | 56

Unashamedly Run! | 59

True North Slope | 61

Vantage Point | 63

A Father's Love | 65

Perfume Station | 68

Velociraptor Experience | 70

Two Steps Closer | 73

Light In, Heavy Out | 75

Valley of Death | 78

Center Punch | 81

Thief of the Woods | 84

Bull with a Bugle Tube | 86

The Art of Waiting | 89

Preseason Prep | 92

Ready At Any Moment | 94

Thermals Rule | 97

Can I Have a Do-Over? | 99

Bibliography | 103

Foreword

For centuries, the outdoors has provided nourishment to body and soul, and throughout history, man has retreated into the wilderness to gain perspective and receive inspiration. Many parallels can be drawn between our experiences in the great outdoors and a deeper meaning of life, and there are many lessons the mountains can teach us about who we are and who we can become.

Since the beginning of time, hunting has provided mankind with sustenance, and hunters have been assigned stewardship of the wildlife and the landscape they inhabit. If we look closely, the outdoors can teach us lessons that will help us be better hunters. If we look closer yet, we will find insight that can help us become better people – better husbands and wives, fathers and mothers. And if we look even more closely, we will discover teachings that will help us become better disciples of Jesus Christ.

Christ himself used parables to illustrate His teachings in the New Testament, using stories that were relatable to people to help teach a higher lesson, to provide deeper understanding. In this book, Brad draws upon his own experiences as a hunter, and through his time spent in the outdoors, shares how these experiences can bring us closer to our Savior and strengthen our faith in Him.

May each of us be inspired by our experiences in the outdoors, and through this book, more frequently seek to connect these experiences to lessons of even greater significance in our lives.

Corey Jacobsen
11-time World Elk Calling Champion

Price of Admission

Whoever wants to be my disciple must deny
themselves and take up their cross and follow me.

(MATT. 16:24)

IN A RECENT POLL, hunters were asked what distance from their parking area they typically hunt. Out of all those surveyed, 88 percent stated they either never or rarely hunt greater than one mile from the vehicle. Whether it be lack of physical ability, unfamiliarity with the ground being hunted, or the ability to locate game near the road, the majority of hunters remain in fairly close proximity to where they park.

I imagine most of us would agree that if we had our way we would prefer to avoid bumping into other hunters in the woods. Having a hunting spot all to yourself undisturbed from other human interference is what we all wish for. However, the physical effort it often takes to achieve that seclusion can mean a huge sacrifice of time and energy. But in my experience, getting deep into the elk woods can be worth every step.

During one particular archery season, the week started off with our hunting party visiting several of our regular haunts. Given we had frequented this part of Oregon many times in the past, our group had identified several feeding and bedding areas that we knew held elk. Unfortunately, due to a growing number of hunters, locations that previously went vastly undisturbed were becoming increasingly filled with more humans and less game. We had to make a change.

After surveying maps and considering various options, our group settled on investigating some new drainages far in the back-country that appeared promising. The terrain featured excellent north-facing slopes, secluded feeding areas, and plenty of water. The only problem was the destination in mind lay four miles from the nearest road.

In order to place ourselves in premium position come first light, our trek required that we be on the trail by 4 a.m. So, with backpacks loaded and headlamps illuminating our way, we began the two-hour predawn journey into the remote wilderness.

The hike was mostly uphill and completely exhausting, but what greeted us was a basin devoid of hunters and teeming with bugling bulls. In fact, the hunting was so good that we endured that same pre-dawn hike day-after-day for the remainder of the week. To steel our resolve for another early morning slog and to remind ourselves of the prize that awaited we began to say that the hike was our "price of admission."

You see, to gain access to undisturbed hunting grounds it was going to cost us something. Our price of admission included loss of sleep, extra miles hiked, elevation gained, and traversing into uncharted territory. Similarly, Jesus warned his followers that there is a cost to being His disciple.

In Luke 14 Jesus spoke bluntly when he stated, "If anyone comes to me and does not hate father and mother, wife and children, brothers and sisters—yes, even their own life—such a person cannot be my disciple" (Luke 14:26). Jesus must become first priority in our lives.

Are you all in with Jesus? In Revelation, a warning was given to those riding the fence: ". . .you are neither hot nor cold. I wish you were either one or the other! So, because you are lukewarm—neither hot nor cold—I am about to spit you out of my mouth" (Rev. 3:15b-16). Jesus's rightful place is on the throne of our hearts. We just simply need to yield control.

Jesus's instructions were clear when He said, "Whoever wants to be my disciple must deny themselves and take up their cross and follow me. For whoever wants to save their life will lose it, but whoever loses their life for me will find it" (Matt. 16:24–25). Whatever you are holding on to, let it go and release it to the Savior. For Jesus has already paid our ultimate "price of admission" on the Cross.

J-Scouting

You will seek me and find me when you
seek me with all your heart.

(Jer. 29:13)

The hunting industry is constantly advancing. As an outdoorsman I always enjoy when our local hunting and sportsman show hits town. All the new products that hit the market every year astonish me—everything from lightweight camo, high-speed archery equipment, advanced optics, or new elk calls—the possibilities to add to my gear collection seem endless.

One recent technological advancement that is gaining considerable interest is E-scouting (or electronic scouting). Services such as Google Earth, Onx Hunt, Go-Hunt Maps and Gaia provide today's outdoor enthusiast with an enormous amount of electronic data right at their fingertips. One of the advantages I enjoy is the ability to pre-plan a portion of my hunt prior to ever putting boots on the ground.

E-scouting allows the outdoorsman to dig into data such as topographical maps, fire burn history, road and trail information, and private vs. public land access. Given the excellent detail of today's mapping software, by the time I ultimately arrive at a new hunt area it almost feels as if I had already visited there. The detail in which today's hunter can prepare with simply a laptop or handheld device is mind boggling.

When we consider our faith journey, can the same thing be said about our time spent J-scouting (or Jesus scouting)? Do we place a higher priority on getting ready for hunting season than we do getting to know our Savior? Jesus wants to know us personally. We are reminded in Revelation, where Jesus says "I stand at the door and knock. If anyone hears my voice and opens the door, I will come in and eat with that person, and they with me" (Rev. 3:20). But we first have to open the door.

I was recently reminded by a pastor friend of mine that Jesus is a gentleman. He will not force His way into our lives. But if we choose to pursue Him the Bible promises we will find Him. Proverbs 8:17 states, "I love those who love me, and those who seek me find me." And in Jeremiah 29:13 we are reminded, "You will seek me and find me when you seek me with all your heart." Jesus wants a personal relationship with each of us.

There are innumerable people who know about Jesus. Some may have learned facts about His life, others have committed a few Bible verses to memory, while others might attend church regularly. Yet they have never allowed the *facts* about Christ to become their personal *reality*. They hold knowledge in their head but no personal relationship in their heart. Jesus warned of such people when he said, "Not everyone who says to me, 'Lord, Lord,' will enter the kingdom of heaven, but only the one who does the will of my Father who is in heaven. . .Then I will tell them plainly, 'I never knew you. Away from me, you evildoers!'" (Mt. 7:21,23).

Just as we use the electronic tools available to prepare us for the next hunt, may we with greater passion, seek to know Jesus better. Whether it be seeking out online teaching from an anointed pastor or perhaps following social media channels that help uplift your faith, take advantage of those sources that can sharpen you! Dive into God's word and allow Him to speak to your spirit. Commit this day to place J-scouting as first priority in your life. God provides us direct access to His throne. Go after Jesus today!

Have To or Get To

So if the Son sets you free, you will be free indeed.
(Jn. 8:36)

ONE OF MY FIRST jobs as a youth was bussing tables at the local buffet restaurant. Not the most glamorous position for a 15-year-old teenager, to be sure. Let's just say, I didn't want my high school buddies to swing by for dinner.

During one particular shift as I was, without a doubt, moping through the motions, my supervisor pulled me aside and offered some timely and wise advice. He simply said, "Do you have to or get to wait on these customers?" That simple yet profound statement has resonated with me from that job to many aspects of my life today. Do I have to or get to?

In many ways, this same principle is applicable each time a hunter steps foot into the backcountry wilderness. You see, elk hunting is often times just plain hard work.

We all expend a vast amount of time, resources, and money preparing for hunting season. The excitement of the first day in elk camp is palpable. And I'll be the first to admit, it's hard to contain my enthusiasm and not walk my legs off on opening day.

But let's face it, by about day three or four once a few blisters have set in, sore muscles abound, and if the hunting has been slow it's easy to talk yourself into a day off. That's the moment I ask myself, "Do I have to or get to?"

Do I have to or get to rise before light to welcome the dawn? Do I have to or get to scale up and down the vast landscape, beholding God's creation all around me? Do I have to or get to experience the majestic elk bugle echoing off the canyon walls?

All too often when I hear non-believers express their views about why they're turned off by Christianity, it seems to center around the perception that "it's just a bunch of rules to follow." As the saying goes, "Don't drink, smoke, chew, or go with girls who do." Much like the Pharisees of Jesus' day, Christianity at times has been relegated to a series of "do's" and "don'ts."

I have good news for you. You can't earn your way into heaven. No matter how many rules you follow, good deeds you perform, or kind acts you carry out toward your brother, none of this will be enough. "For it is by grace you have been saved through faith—and this is not from yourselves, it is the gift of God—not by works, so that no one can boast" (Eph. 2:8–9). Jesus has already paid the ultimate price. Nothing we can do through our own efforts can earn our salvation. Good works should be the result of Christ's love working through us, not a means for us to try and earn His favor.

Don't get me wrong, we should all strive to do good, as loving your neighbor as yourself is one of God's greatest commandments. But our salvation cannot be bought through anything we might accomplish. Jesus has already performed all the work through His death on the Cross. We just simply get to receive His free gift of redemption.

Living for Christ is not a "have to" but a "get to." As we are reminded in Romans, "For what the law was powerless to do. . ., God did by sending His own Son. . ." (Rom 8:3). We get to trust in Jesus. We get to live in freedom. We get to experience peace amidst the chaos. And we get to simply rest in His presence.

It's time to flip our thinking and take on a Christ-centered "get to" mindset. Live in the freedom Jesus offers today.

Read The Signs

Who do you say I am?

(Mt. 16:15)

Are you like me and guilty of occasionally leaving the house a little unkept when your spouse leaves town? I'm not sure what your typical home life looks like but my wife, Michele, and I enjoy keeping a fairly tidy place. However, I must admit, when Michele leaves on a trip for a few days I've been known to let some daily chores slide. You might find an unmade bed, dirty dishes in the sink, or the trash needing to be taken out. The key is knowing when your spouse is coming home, right?

Within a few hours of my wife's return, I am likely scurrying around the house picking up, wiping down, and vacuuming, attempting to return the house to how she remembered it. The only problem is there are often signs left behind that find me guilty. My wife knows me too well!

One of the things I love about elk hunting is the challenge of the pursuit. Reading the clues left behind of where the elk have been and where they're moving is part of the chase. Examining elk droppings, well-used game trails, bull rubs, or wallows are just some of the signs that might provide us with information on where to focus our energies.

The goal is to, of course, use our time as wisely and as efficiently as possible anytime we step foot in the woods. Effective elk hunting often requires covering ground and putting miles behind you to determine where the elk are living. But once you find that "sweet spot" where the signs are plentiful, you can be confident the elk are likely nearby, and the hunt is on!

In Jesus' day, the Israelites were looking for the signs of His coming. During a time of Roman rule, the Jewish nation was searching for their long-awaited Savior, someone who would save and free them from their oppression. However, Jesus had a different aim in mind when He stated, ". . .the Son of Man did not come to be served, but to serve, and to give his life as a ransom for many" (Mt. 20:28). He came to be a servant leader.

With all the controversy surrounding Jesus—Pharisees ridiculing Him, crowds questioning Him, followers requesting signs and miracles—Jesus asked His disciples a simple yet vitally important question, "Who do you say I am?" Simon Peter responded, "You are the Messiah, the Son of the living God" (Mt. 16:15–16). This is a question that each of us must answer.

Evidence That Demands a Verdict by Josh McDowell was one of the most influential books during my formative years as a young Christian. In that book, Dr. McDowell investigated whether there is evidence for believing the Bible is true and was Jesus truly who He said He was. The book goes on to highlight fact after fact concerning recorded evidence, eyewitness accounts, ancient literature, and fulfilled prophecy, making the case for Christ. In the end, the "signs" or facts about Jesus being who he said he was are irrefutable.

The question Dr. McDowell's book posed is the same one people continue to ask today—was Jesus a liar, lunatic, or Lord?[1] This question was settled in my heart and mind when I accepted Christ. But each person must come to a conclusion concerning that same question in their own lives. Jesus doesn't leave any room for a middle ground.

I pray today that if you haven't already, you would "read the signs" around you, consider the evidence in scripture, and choose Jesus.

---

1. McDowell, *Evidence That Demands a Verdict*, 25.

Failure Is an Option

*For though the righteous fall seven times, they rise
again, but the wicked stumble when calamity strikes.*
(Pv. 24:16)

As HARD AS WE might try, we all experience failure in life. A failed driver's test, exam questions missed, mistakes made at work, the list goes on. Although failure can seem disappointing in the moment, ultimately our mistakes can lead to some of life's greatest lessons. Thomas Edison famously stated, "I have not failed. I have found 10,000 ways that don't work."[1] True failure is not making mistakes but the unwillingness to get back up and keep trying.

If disappointments experienced in the woods correlated with my motivation for returning the next hunting season I would have given up a long time ago, as my failures have been too numerous to count. For instance, the time I mistakenly touched my bow release as I was drawing back on a bull, launching my arrow 50 feet over its back. Or accidentally ranging the tree behind an elk instead of the animal itself causing me to misjudge the yardage and use the wrong sight pin. Experiences from freezing up in the heat of the moment, breaking a branch during a quiet stalk, or forgetting to factor the wind direction while approaching my target have all served as disappointments and failures. The question for us all is how do we respond to those failures.

1. Edison Innovation Foundation, "Importance of Thomas Edison Quotes."

During the tenuous Apollo 13 landing mission, NASA flight director Gene Kranz was quoted as saying, "Failure is not an option."[2] However, I would submit that taking the complete opposite mindset while hunting is vital. Failure *is* an option!

I understand none of us wish to fail. We all want to fill the tag in our pocket each time we embark on a hunt. Yet it's the numerous lessons I've learned over the years from failure rather than success that have resulted in my becoming a better hunter. It's the response we take to mistakes and missed opportunities that is key.

Do you get dejected and head back to camp? Do you allow yourself to get frustrated and lose concentration? Have you hosted your own pity party in the woods, only to lose out on future opportunities in the process? Or have you simply given up, packed up camp early, and headed home? These are often our natural responses to failure. Yet if you take the proper mindset, failed opportunities can not only be times of learning how to be a better hunter but also moments of growth in maturity, discipline, and overcoming adversity in life.

When you carefully examine scripture, you will notice it is chock full of characters that experienced failure. From the very beginning of mankind, Adam and Eve failed to obey God's specific restrictions. Or the example in 2 Samuel of King David, described as a "man after God's own heart," who committed both adultery and murder. And even the apostle Peter, one of Jesus' own disciples, denied his Savior three times (Mt. 26). From a spiritual perspective, God knows we will all sin. The scripture teaches, "We all, like sheep, have gone astray, each of us has turned to our own way. . ." (Is. 53:6a). No one is immune. Only Jesus is perfect and without sin.

One of the things that helps us relate to Jesus as a personal Savior is that He has walked in our shoes. Hebrews 4:15 teaches, "For we do not have a high priest who is unable to empathize with our weaknesses, but we have one who has been tempted in every way, just as we are—yet he did not sin." Jesus understands our troubles, temptations, and failures. John 16:33 reads, "In this

2. Smithsonian National Air & Space Museum, "Multimedia Gallery."

world you will have trouble. But take heart! I have overcome the world." Jesus has provided a way out for you and me.

So as you walk this Christian journey, be reminded today that you have a Savior who understands your sin and struggles. Failure is not only an option but a reality for all of us. "For all have sinned and fall short of the glory of God" (Rom. 3:23). But Jesus is the solution. He promises, "as far as the east is from the west, so far has he removed our transgressions from us" (Ps. 103:12). No sin is too deep, no mistake too severe that Jesus won't forgive.

I challenge you to take a moment and really examine your life. Open up your hearts and allow Jesus to scour those hidden places. Place your sins at the foot of the Cross. For our God is faithful to forgive. Turn your past failures into victory through Christ today!

When in Doubt Walk it Out

*Give careful thought to the paths for your feet and
be steadfast in all your ways. Do not turn to the
right or the left; keep your foot from evil.*

(Pv. 4:26–27)

I OFTEN DO MY best thinking when I'm exercising. Something about getting the blood pumping seems to stimulate the neurons in my brain and heightens my mental awareness. If I need to ponder on a decision, my wife will attest that you can usually find me walking laps around the property at our home.

With elk hunting I typically take the same approach. During a recent September trip I had the privilege to hunt multiple states in Utah and Idaho. Given both units were new to our hunting party, the plan was to put miles behind us and cover significant ground to not only learn the topography, but more importantly to locate bulls.

Although it doesn't take much to get me pumped up about elk hunting, opening day of season offers a special kind of allure. Despite my best efforts to tamp down the excitement, it's not uncommon for me to walk my legs off the first day out. On this particular hunt, after consulting my son's Garmin watch following our initial jaunt into the backcountry, I realized our enthusiasm had again won out. For 16 miles and 4,100 feet of elevation later, we had officially broken in our hiking boots!

As the next two weeks would unfold, the mantra of "when in doubt walk it out" became our rallying cry. Fording streams, climbing canyons, negotiating basins, and side hilling ridge after ridge, we covered miles in search of our elusive quarry. No one would accuse us of not putting in an honest effort. For at the end of our two weeks the statistics bore out as to how my body felt. We had covered nearly 200 miles with over 30,000 feet of elevation climbed.

Martin Luther was quoted as saying, "A Christian is never in a state of completion but always in the process of becoming."[1] The longer I have been a Christian, the more this statement rings true. As I reflect back on my faith journey, specific points along the path stand out where God used His refining tools to chip away those rough edges in my life.

Once we accept Christ, this is just the start of the journey. It's a daily walk with our Savior. The important piece is having the willingness to be molded and changed. For each of us this refining process can look different. For some the rough edges might be dealing with dishonesty, others filthy language, and still others might struggle with overcoming temptation regarding pornography. It doesn't matter what the sin. For the Scripture says, "all have sinned and fall short of the glory of God" (Rm. 3:23). The key is having the desire to become more and more like Jesus.

My encouragement for you today as you walk this Christian journey is this, invite God's Holy Spirit to scour every nook and cranny of your soul. Strive to live more and more like Jesus that the world will see Christ in your life. For as Billy Graham was quoted as saying, "We're the Bibles the world is reading; we are the creeds the world is needing; we are the sermons the world is heeding."[2]

When you reach the end of your Christian journey and God takes an accounting from your "Garmin faith watch," how many miles will it say you walked? How many ridges did you climb? Did you give it everything you had? As you continue to walk out your faith, my prayer is that Jesus shine more brightly through your life each day. Keep striving after God, place your full trust in Him, and He will guide your every step.

1. Minimalist Quotes, "Martin Luther Quotes."
2. Goodreads, "Billy Graham Quotes."

No Plan B

I am the way and the truth and the life. No one comes to the Father except through me.

(JN. 14:6)

WITHOUT CONSCIOUSLY THINKING ABOUT it, we all make a multitude of choices every day. Some may be small such as what we choose to eat for lunch, the e-mail messages we'll respond to that day, or how fast we choose to drive to work. In contrast, decisions concerning who we decide to marry, the college we attend, our vocation, or the location in which we decide to live can have much larger life-altering implications. Whether big or small, our choices help guide our life's path.

Anyone who has stepped into the woods sympathizes with the challenge of deciding where to hunt on any given day. How many times have you sat around camp trying to decide between a multitude of hunt choices? Should we hunt low or high today, walk up from the trailhead or cut cross-country, or sit quietly on a meadow versus walking ridgebacks? The choices can seem endless.

As the years have gone by, I have made a point to prepare multiple hunt plans before ever leaving the house. With the advent of digital scouting, I can now scout and map out several different options in advance from the comfort of my own home. I like to have Plan A, B, C, and D!

During one particular year, all of our preseason scouting had indicated that the best hunting would be found at higher altitudes.

With fresh game trails, elk rubs, and feed abounding in this elevation band, we were confident our primary hunt plan was spot on. However, it wasn't until a few actual hard hunting days were behind us that we realized our original intel was faulty. The elk had moved and we needed to make a change too.

Fortunately for us we had prepared a Plan B. By making a significant shift in both elevation and habitat, it didn't take long until we were thick into the elk. The bulls were bugling and the hunting for the remainder of the week was lively and intense. All because we had a back-up plan.

The world would like you to think there are multiple ways to heaven. If I'm loving toward my neighbor, give generously to charity, feed the hungry, and obey the laws of the land the world says I can earn my way into God's favor. Although these are all indeed good, the Bible is abundantly clear that God prepared only one path into His kingdom and that is through belief in His one and only son, Jesus. We cannot earn our salvation.

Jesus spoke of himself this way when he said, "I am the gate; whoever enters through me will be saved" (Jn. 10:9a). The book of John also describes God's perfect plan for humanity when it states, "For God so loved the world that he gave his one and only Son, that whoever believes in him shall not perish but have eternal life" (Jn. 3:16). Jesus has made a way for each of us; it is His ultimate and perfect plan, if we only choose to believe.

Unlike different hunt options while in the woods, there is only one way to heaven. Teaching his disciples, Jesus stated, "I am the way and the truth and the life. No one comes to the Father except through me" (Jn. 14:6).

Just as Joshua posed a timeless question to the Israelites following their deliverance from the Egyptians in asking the people, ". . .choose for yourselves this day whom you will serve. . .," we too must answer this same question in our own hearts and lives. My prayer is that you might answer as Joshua did, "But as for me and my household, we will serve the Lord" (Js. 24:15). For in God's blueprint there is no Plan B.

Two Better Than One

As iron sharpens iron, so one person sharpens another.
(PROV. 27:17)

IN CORPORATE AMERICA IT'S a dog-eat-dog world. Positioning yourself ahead of the next person to ensure you come out on top is encouraged. A "me first" mentality exists where there's only one winner, and that winner must be you.

In stark contrast, success in elk hunting often requires reliance on a hunting partner, someone you can team with to not only call elk, but a person with whom you can share the overall experience. A confidant that shares your struggles as you slog up a ridgeback, a friend that welcomes the rising sun in the East, or a buddy that helps pack out a heavy load of meat—for me, hunting is an experience that is better shared.

I have been fortunate to have had several great hunting partners over the years. Getting the opportunity to tag along with my dad during my formative years can never be replaced. In hindsight, I'm sure my inexperience led to several lost opportunities for him but the time spent in the woods together was a precious gift. As years have passed, sharing the hunt with my three boys, Caleb, Kyle, and Lucas, my brother Doug, and several other good friends have made my hunting experiences all the more enjoyable and memorable.

There is something within the struggle that is difficult to explain to a non-hunter. But when the adversity can be shared, the bonds formed reach deep. Much in the same way, God did not intend for the Christian to walk this journey alone. In Hebrews, the writer encourages us to "let us consider how we may spur one another on toward love and good deeds, not giving up meeting together" (Heb. 10:24–25). God created us for community, to share one another's burdens.

The Bible also encourages the believer to "pray for each other" (Jm. 5:16). Having an accountability partner in your life with whom you can be real and share your deepest needs, struggles, or victories cannot be matched. A friend that can encourage you when you're down, affirm you through scripture, correct you when you're going off track, or provide godly perspective as you face life's challenges is invaluable.

Is there someone in your life right now that you can confide in? If yes, take time to thank God for this person. The gift of a brother or sister in Christ makes this journey in life so much sweeter. King Soloman understood this principle when he wrote, "As iron sharpens iron, so one person sharpens another" (Prov. 27:17). Examine those people in your circle of influence. If you don't have one already, pray that God would bring a Christian friend into your life. Surround yourself with like-minded people and don't walk this Christian life alone. Two are better than one.

Game Trails

*In all your ways submit to him, and he
will make your paths straight.*

(Pv. 3:6)

DON'T WE ALL TEND to take the path of least resistance? Water flows downhill for a reason! We as humans often search for efficiencies, shortcuts, and the easiest route in accomplishing a task. If you have a 'honey-do checklist,' isn't it customary to tick off the easiest or least time-consuming items first? This just seems to be normal human behavior.

As I have spent numerous hours in the woods, game trails never cease to amaze me. They are like an organized animal highway with intersections and turnoffs, all instinctively created to allow game to move through the landscape efficiently. Animals, like humans, will look for that same path of least resistance. If they can limit their exertion by avoiding obstacles and follow the natural contours of the terrain they will.

While pursuing elk, I tend to analyze game trails carefully. If you pay attention to indicators such as size of hoof prints, directionality of travel, and overall usage, game trails can provide guidance as to where to next focus your efforts. They can often point the hunter toward feeding or bedding areas or in the case of old, unused trails, hunt areas to avoid.

Hunting along a well-used game trail also serves as a nice method to move across the landscape. I personally love how quiet and stealthy a well-worn game trail allows us to be as we stalk our prey. I remember one instance when a group of bedded elk were located on a secluded bench 100 yards above me. Although the terrain around my location was crunchy and dry, by using the animal highway as I crept within bow range, I was able to move inside 30 yards undetected. In that case, the elk's reliance on the well-worn path was its undoing.

My senior year in college served as a turning point in my Christian faith. It was during a chapel revival service where the speaker challenged us students to "go against the flow," to willingly resist cultural norms and the current trends of the day just because they're popular. Avoid taking the path of least resistance but rather, commit your whole self to Christ—mind, body, and spirit, holding nothing back. Go all in with Jesus no matter what the cost. A spiritual step called sanctification.

You see, as Christians, you and I are called to be in the world but not of the world. As Romans 12:2 says, "Do not conform to the pattern of this world, but be transformed by the renewing of your mind. Then you will be able to test and approve what God's will is—his good, pleasing and perfect will."

I would like to believe my thinking is sound. Yet if I don't allow the Holy Spirit to permeate my mind and take captive every thought, I am destined to be led astray! As Proverbs 14:12 warns, "There is a way that appears to be right, but in the end it leads to death." May we allow God to sanctify our thoughts.

Each of us has only limited time on this earth. Let's make a stand today to follow God no matter the cost. May we follow Job's example as he proclaimed, "My feet have closely followed his steps, I have kept to his way without turning aside" (Jb 23:11).

Allow God to set your course. Get into God's word and seek His direction. Don't follow the easy path—the "game trail of life" that may lead to your destruction. Instead, allow yourself to be led by God even when the path seems difficult. The final destination is worth it!

Get Your Sights Right

Let us fix our eyes on Jesus, the author
and perfector of our faith...

(HEB. 12:2A)

HISTORICALLY, DESPITE MY LOVE for hunting, I have remained somewhat of a tightwad when it comes to purchasing new equipment. Unlike one of my hunting partners who purchases so much new gear we have affectionately nicknamed him the "walking Cabela's catalog," I have a tendency to use the same gear year after year. However, one particular season I finally succumbed and invested in a new set of fiber optic sights for my archery set-up, as the pins in my old system were becoming increasingly hard to see in low-light situations. Oh, how this minor upgrade would come back to haunt me!

On September 10th, the opening day of our hunt, my brother and I made a brief motorcycle ride to the trailhead down a bumpy, pothole-filled, gravel Forest Service road. From the trailhead we dropped over the ridgetop into some of Oregon's premier elk country. As we descended a grueling 2000 feet into the valley below, fresh sign of rutting bulls was clearly evident. It didn't take long before we heard our first elk bugle of the season and the game was on.

Moving quickly, my brother set up to call as I positioned myself fifty yards forward near an old growth stump. An exchange of bugles continued for the next twenty minutes until finally the bull had heard enough. The once lifeless brush below my position began to sway and I watched in disbelief as a giant set of antlers suddenly materialized above the foliage. The herd bull, a beautiful 6x6, was headed straight in my direction!

As my heart pounded out of my chest, I somehow fumbled with my rangefinder to identify yardages of a few trees nearby. In almost scripted fashion, the bull turned broadside looking uphill towards my brother's location without any knowledge of my presence. Thirty yards on the money, standing still, the bull of my dreams! The many hours of practice and pursuit were finally going to pay off.

I silently drew back my bow, settled the 30-yard pin behind the bull's front shoulder, and fired. It was like slow motion, watching the arrow track its precise course. With full anticipation of a lethal impact, I was jarred back to reality as I watched my arrow sail harmlessly three feet over the bull's back. What had just happened? Was this a dream?

After returning to camp, I tried another shot at the practice target and again missed three feet high. While bouncing down the road on my motorcycle, to my shock and horror, the screw mechanism on my new sights had come loose, sliding my sight pins to the bottom of the housing. In archery terms, my 30-yard pin had just become a 100-yard shot!

None of us are exempt from experiencing disappointment. Despite the most careful and meticulous planning, we cannot control our circumstances. Yet amidst our disappointments in life, a few biblical truths resonate. First, when disappointment hits, do not sin! The Psalmist encourages us "In your anger do not sin; when you are on your beds, search your hearts and be silent" (Ps. 4:4). We can choose to worship God in the midst of the trial. Worshiping God while we're disappointed allows us to see the hope He has for us, even though we may not fully understand His plans at that moment.

Second, disappointments allow the believer to develop a deeper trust in God if we keep our sights set on the knowledge that He has our best in mind. Proverbs reminds us, "In his heart a man plans his course, but the Lord determines his steps" (Prov. 16:9). We all want to understand why we experience what we do. Maybe you have struggled with a rebellious teenager, troubled marriage, loss of a job, or are battling disease—the list goes on. But we can rest in the promise that God will never leave us through the trial. The Bible promises, "neither height nor depth, nor anything else in all creation, will be able to separate us from the love of God that is in Christ Jesus our Lord" (Rom 8:39).

Finally, disappointment helps us "get our sights right." When trouble comes, our focus can so often turn to the world around us. But instead, "Let us fix our eyes on Jesus, the author and perfecter of our faith, who for the joy set before him endured the cross, scorning its shame, and sat down at the right hand of the throne of God" (Heb. 12:2). Pray today for God's recalibration of your sights. Keep a laser-beamed focus on Him, that you may experience life through Jesus' eyes.

Bugle Fest Interloper

*See that you are not led astray. For many will
come in my name, saying "I am he!" and "The
time is at hand!" Do not go after them.*

(Lk 21:8 ESV)

THE AIR WAS CRISP and cold. September leaves were turning as
we traversed along a finger ridge, descending our way towards
the creek bottom below. With the orange glow of the coming day
approaching, my brother Doug and I, along with our eldest sons,
Caleb and Ryan, hiked deep into elk country.

If bulls can be located before first light, the complete trajectory of the day can be affected. So it was on this fall morning. As
the first locator bugle was cast into the fog-covered basin, our ears
were met with a chorus of multiple responses cascading back from
the canyon below. A "bugle fest" had begun and we had our pick
of the litter.

We agreed together to go after the bull that broadcasted a
particularly deep, gravelly bugle. Not wasting time, we quickly descended toward the valley floor, moving to within 200 yards of the
last known response. As Ryan and I stayed behind to call, Caleb
and Doug began to close the distance.

Starting with a short locator bugle, it didn't take long before
our bull was screaming directly across the drainage. With each
consecutive challenge the bugling only intensified, and we could

tell this bull was ready for a fight. Not wanting to disappoint our challenger, the showdown commenced.

Over the years, we have experimented with various elk calling tactics. One of our more successful methods has involved the caller keeping the bull preoccupied and vocal while the shooter stalks in quietly using the bull's intermittent bugles as a locator beacon. If we are able to keep the wind right, more often than not the shooter can move into bow range without detection. The problem during this particular set-up was the intrusion of what we begrudgingly named the "bugle fest interloper."

You see, as Doug and Caleb were stealthily moving up below our bugling bull, it turns out another visitor was also watching the action. From the corner of his eye, Caleb caught a dark outline on the pine tree directly adjacent to his position. A black bear was shimmying down the trunk of the tree a mere 17 yards away.

Momentarily forgetting about the bull and more concerned with their immediate safety, Caleb instinctively drew and fired. With his expandable broadhead striking true, the bear didn't make it far. Unfortunately, with the ensuing noise and commotion the hunt for our true prize was all but over.

What distracts you from God? It seems our lives are constantly bombarded by diversions and temptations that aim to pull us away and drag us down. We react instinctively rather than prayerfully. In Galatians 5, scripture describes this conflict as a struggle between walking "by the Spirit" or satisfying the "desires of the flesh." It goes on to say, "For the flesh desires what is contrary to the Spirit, and the Spirit what is contrary to the flesh. They are in conflict with each other. . ." (Gal. 5:16–17).

Jesus understood temptation. While in the garden of Gethsemane, despite their best intentions and even though Jesus warned his disciples that, "The spirit is willing, but the flesh is weak" (Matt. 26:41) the disciples fell asleep. The Bible goes on to offer us clear warnings of the "acts of the flesh" to avoid, such as sexual immorality, impurity, hatred, fits of rage, drunkenness, and the like. (Gal 5:19–21). But thanks be to God He has provided a way for us to overcome those daily temptations through life in the Spirit.

We have protection against the devil and his schemes. For every believer there is the promise of the full armor of God, to withstand any of the enemy's attacks. Satan wants to deceive us, distract us, and pull us away from the true prize that awaits us in Christ.

Don't allow the distractions of this world to divert your attention. But instead, fix your "eyes on Jesus, the pioneer and perfecter of faith" (Heb. 12:2). Guard your heart and mind from the "bugle fest interloper" of our souls. For if we stand to the end, the treasure that awaits is worth it all.

No Day Wasted

Whatever you do, work at it with all your heart, as working for the Lord, not for human masters. . .

(Col. 3:23)

At the end of the day, don't we all want our lives to count for something? When they read your obituary isn't it important that you did more than simply consume oxygen and die? Don't we all long for purpose and meaning in our lives? As the saying goes, "One day your life will flash before your eyes. Make sure it's worth watching."[1]

I love this life God has blessed me with and desire to live it to the fullest. This mindset trickles over into my approach to hunting. Considering archery is my typical weapon of choice, elk season in my home state of Oregon is limited to a mere 30 days. For rifle hunters, their season is shorter yet. I, like many, have only limited vacation days and time to be away from family, so once I make it to hunting camp my goal is to make each day count. No day wasted!

My wife thinks I'm a little crazy, but more than once I've been known to drive through the night to elk camp. In an effort to maximize every hunting day possible, I recall one season leaving immediately after the final horn sounded following the conclusion of my son's Friday night football game. With my truck loaded to the hilt I trekked the 460 miles thru the pitch-black night, arriving at camp just as orange tinted the eastern horizon. Although running

1. Quotefancy, "Edward Way Quotes."

on zero sleep, adrenaline ran high as I was afforded a bonus morning hunt for my efforts.

I don't mean to imply the false narrative that I never take days off. Certainly we need to listen to our bodies and provide rest when necessary. But as a general rule, my hunting philosophy is to show up, be on time, utilize the time available, and hunt hard! We wait all year for this opportunity so let's not waste it. It's tempting to stay in bed when we're tired, cold, or simply discouraged. But through putting in the extra effort to strap on my gear each day, I am constantly blown away by the wilderness God created for us to enjoy.

As we consider our approach to daily living, the Word of God shows that Christ is concerned about our daily decisions and practical lives. Ephesians 5:15–17 instructs the believer, "Be very careful, then, how you live—not as unwise but as wise, making the most of every opportunity, because the days are evil. Therefore, do not be foolish, but understand what the Lord's will is." You see, our choices matter! God wishes for each of us to live a full life, living squarely in the middle of His will during our time on this earth. We can accomplish this only through knowing and following Him.

Although Jesus is no longer with us in bodily form, He left us an example of how to live. Furthermore, Christ gave each believer their marching orders when He stated, ". . .Go into all the world and preach the gospel to all creation" (Mk. 16:15). We are all Christ's ambassadors. He didn't leave this work solely to your pastor at church. God has called each of us to action, wishing to make His appeal to an unbelieving world through us.

When you think about your life in that context, it brings a different perspective to how we approach each day. We have been called to be the hands and feet of Jesus. Christ left us the example when He taught His disciples, "For even the Son of Man did not come to be served, but to serve. . ." (Mk. 10:45a). We should go and do likewise.

So as we approach a new day, let's strive to make every moment count. May our lives represent the One in whom we place our trust. Let's make a conscious choice to, as Jesus demonstrated, serve others as we would wish to be served. The choice is ours. Commit today to "No Day Wasted."

Attitude Adjustment

*The Lord himself goes before you and will be with
you; he will never leave you nor forsake you.
Do not be afraid; do not be discouraged.*

(DEUT. 31:8)

THERE'S A LOT TO be said about maintaining a positive attitude. In fact, medical studies reveal several health benefits directly linked to positive thinking. Lower rates of depression, decreased levels of distress and pain, and greater resistance to illness have all been associated with those who uphold an optimistic outlook on life. In short, we become healthier, happier, and more hopeful.

My best friend growing up came from a family of all boys— eight to be exact. With my buddy born squarely in the middle, he had younger brothers to tease but plenty of older siblings who wouldn't hesitate to put him in his place. Anytime I had a sleepover at his house it was like survival of the fittest. It goes without saying that there was plenty of testosterone flowing and multiple opportunities to show who was king of the hill.

As you might imagine, it was commonplace to sustain a few bumps and bruises during our forays with his brothers. But I learned early on there wasn't much mercy given for whining about it. Unless you needed stitches or nearly had an extremity missing, my friend's dad delivered a familiar response each time we thought we were hurt by saying, "It's a long way from your heart." I guess he figured with eight boys, he needed to parent a little from the school of hard knocks. In other words, quit complaining, brush it off, and get an attitude adjustment.

With elk hunting, if you're not careful about your attitude, it's easy to become discouraged. Elk are large yet elusive animals. They are built to cover large distances, they possess keen senses to danger, and often take shelter in hard-to-reach places, making hunting them a challenging endeavor. To compound matters, as elk hunters we often work our tails off to get an opportunity for a shot only to have some small factor—wind change, noise, movement—blow up our chance. Keeping a positive mental frame of mind can be difficult.

It's a running joke in our hunting camp about our numerous failures in the woods. Instead of writing these pages as a devotional book, my three boys have teasingly prodded that I have enough stories to write a hunting bloopers book. If I allowed a failure or two to dominate my thinking, it would be easy to take a day off, sleep in, or simply give up and stay home. Yet to the best of my ability, I have strived to use failures as learning opportunities, attempting to maintain a positive outlook toward the next hunt.

We all experience discouragement in life. It could be the loss of a job, poor performance on a test, or a failed relationship. These times can certainly leave us feeling drained, alone, or simply exhausted. But we can take solace in the knowledge that God hears our cry for help. "The righteous cry out, and the Lord hears them; he delivers them from all their troubles." (Ps. 34:17) During difficult situations, we are also invited to place our worries before God. Psalms 55:22 admonishes, "Cast your cares on the Lord and he will sustain you; he will never let the righteous be shaken."

So, let's strive to turn our discouragement into encouragement. By taking on a heart of thankfulness for our blessings, focusing on what we get to experience in the outdoors and God's goodness in our lives, we can change our perspective. Take time to appreciate the small things you've been given and let's enjoy the journey. A positive attitude adjustment can be all it takes.

Tell Me Your Stories, Boys

*This is the confidence we have in approaching God: that
if we ask anything according to his will, he hears us.*

(1 Jn. 5:14)

There was no greater joy for my wife and myself than when
our kids came home from school and couldn't wait to tell us about
their day. They wanted to tell us their stories. Don't we all want to
be heard? The Greek philosopher Epictetus was attributed as saying, "We have two ears and one mouth so that we can listen twice
as much as we speak."[1] There is power in hearing someone's stories.

I believe being a good listener can often be taken for granted.
You see, effective listening requires attention to the speaker. When
someone listens as you talk, it shows that your ideas and feelings
are being acknowledged and you have something important to say.
My dad fit that mold.

For the last 15 years of his life, my dad served as hunting camp
host. For most of my lifetime he was a "dyed in the wool" hunter,
but sadly age and health issues forced him out of the woods. But
he never wanted to miss hunting camp. While his boys, grandsons,
and good friends would go hunting for the day, dad would tend the
campsite, enjoy his own quiet time with God, and always have the
coffee on when we arrived back, waiting with anticipation to hear
about our hunt. His voice still resonates to this day as he spoke,
"Tell me your stories, boys!"

1. Brainy Quote, "Epictetus Quotes."

Dad would want to hear all the details. "Where did you hunt? Did you see anything? Were the bulls bugling? Any shot opportunities?" My dad loved everything there was about hunting and could live vicariously through our stories. Many times you may have felt you didn't even have a story to tell yet he would continue to probe until you shared something he could rejoice with you about. My dad was a great listener.

Everyone reading these words has a story to tell. Beyond the realm of hunting we each have our own unique life narrative. Where you were raised, family make-up, important life decisions, or major influencers in your life all contribute to each of our life stories.

Have you ever stopped to realize that your story is important to God? The God of the universe knows you inside and out for He created you, knowing you even before you were born. "Before I formed you in the womb I knew you, before you were born I set you apart. . ." (Jer. 1:15). No one is an accident. As King David proclaimed, "I praise you because I am fearfully and wonderfully made; your works are wonderful, I know that full well" (Ps. 139:14). Each of us is important to God.

In the same way, God's story is important to us. The full account of history from God's "very good" creation, to the fall, to Christ's redemption and ultimate reconciliation of humanity with our Savior, the Bible contains the storyboard of God's plan for humanity. For God's story includes both you and me. As 2 Peter 3:9b states, ". . .he is patient with you, not wanting anyone to perish, but everyone to come to repentance." The Bible is ultimately a chronicle about God's redemptive plan for all mankind.

So the most important question still remains. Do you know His story? God has given us His written Word that we may know Him personally—who He is, what He has done for us, and what we can have through Him. God longs for a personal relationship with you and me and wants to hear from His children.

My challenge to you today is return to that childlike faith. As Jesus stated, "Truly I tell you, unless you change and become like little children, you will never enter the kingdom of heaven" (Mt.

18:3). If you don't already, get to know God's story. Be vulnerable and tell your story to God. Akin to my dad sitting in camp waiting to say, "Tell me your stories, boys," God is patiently waiting to hear from you and me. Open up your heart and allow God to complete your life story today.

Boots on the Ground

. . .whatever you did for one the least of these
brothers and sisters of mine, you did for me.

(MT. 25:40)

THERE'S NOTHING LIKE REAL-LIFE lessons. Much like attending a college or technical school, while in training we acquire a significant amount of head knowledge. But until we take what was learned and practically apply it, it's difficult to fully understand all the intricacies of the job.

The same can be said when it comes to elk hunting new country. We can be as prepared as possible through pre-hunt planning, e-scouting, talking to others who have hunted the area, or consulting historical hunting statistics for our target unit. However, until you place "boots on the ground" and actually walk the landscape, it's difficult to gain a full appreciation of what you're getting into. Head knowledge can never replace experience.

So it was for a new hunting location that has since been playfully nicknamed "suicide ridge." After consulting numerous maps and hunting software, a promising north facing slope was identified that appeared likely to hold game. Although I was familiar with the general hunt area, this particular canyon face was new to me. Oh, the surprise that awaited.

With great anticipation and as first light approached, I had positioned myself squarely at the top of the 2,500-foot-tall ridgeback. It didn't take long after casting my first locator bugle before

I received the high-pitched response from a bull in the valley below. It was time to close the distance. However, my knees were rudely awakened as I began to make my initial descent down the steep pitch of the mountain face. With the slope being much more severe than first anticipated, traversing downhill felt more like a controlled slide versus a hike. What I envisioned the country to look like from my scouting was vastly different in real time.

As a good hunter, I couldn't stop now. So, with steeled resolve, I continued the grueling descent to the bull's location. The problem was the mountain pitch wasn't decreasing but rather increasing in severity. Grabbing at bushes and tree branches, I finally arrived at the elk's elevation only to be busted by a change in the wind. I had dropped more than 2,000 feet over the steep canyon face with only one way back to camp. . . up. Suicide ridge lived up to its name.

In Jesus' day, the Pharisees were confronted for their hypocrisy. For as teachers of the law, they possessed head knowledge of Old Testament scripture but no heart transformation. As the religious leaders of their day, the Pharisees had all the rules and regulations memorized yet "neglected the more important matters of the law—justice, mercy and faithfulness." (Mt. 23:23) Jesus went on describe them as "whitewashed tombs, which look beautiful on the outside but on the inside are full of the bones of the dead. . ." (Mt. 23:27).

Jesus calls His followers to action. It's one thing to know the Scriptures and another to practically live out God's calling in our lives. The writer of the book of James warns the believer, "Do not merely listen to the word, and so deceive yourselves. Do what it says." (Jm 1:22). God is calling each of us to put "boots on the ground" as we live out our faith.

As Christ's disciples we are His representatives to the world around us. Jesus described our influence as such when he stated, "You are the salt of the earth" (Mt. 5:13a) and "You are the light of the world" (Mt. 5:14a).

He has called us to action. We are challenged to love our neighbors (Mk. 12:31), take care of the poor (Deut. 15:11), feed the hungry (Is. 58:10), clothe the needy (1 Jn. 3:17), and be hospitable to strangers (Mt. 25:35). There is no such thing as a passive Christian.

As Benjamin Franklin famously stated, "A well done is better than a well said."[1] There are needs all around us and the world is watching. So as you walk the next ridgeback, ford the adjacent stream, or hike the next steep ridge during your hunting season, may your "boots on the ground" remind you of practical steps you can take as you put faith into action.

1. The Franklin Institute, "Benjamin Franklin Famous Quotes," line 9.

Blood Trail

. . .the blood of Jesus, his Son, purifies us from all sin.

(1 Jn. 1:7b)

A FAMOUS HISTORIAN AND scientist was quoted as saying, "Blood is a very special juice."[1] Unbelievably, the heart pumps 63 million gallons of blood in our lifetime. Blood carries all the essential nutrients and oxygen to our cells. We manufacture 17 million red blood cells every second. When we're injured, our blood even clots to prevent us from bleeding to death. Blood is truly a vital component of life.

We all need blood to survive. Unlike being able to get an artificial joint replacement or even a mechanical heart, there is no such thing as artificial blood. Blood gives life.

As hunters, we take the shedding of an animal's blood seriously. We realize through the taking of a game animal's life it contains sustenance and provision for us and our families. Following a blood trail to its conclusion is a sacred moment and one I never take lightly.

One memorable blood trail occurred during my youth as I accompanied my dad on a hunt. Although we were primarily hunting elk, dad also carried a deer tag in his pocket. On this particular morning, as we rounded a stand of timber, a forked horn mule deer grazed undisturbed 50 yards ahead. In his excitement, my

1. Wolfgang von Goethe, *Faust*, 135.

dad drew and fired a little too quickly, jerking his archery equipment left and appearing to completely miss the animal.

While retrieving his arrow from the distant embankment, we were both shocked to find a sliver of blood on one solitary blade of his 4-blade broadhead. In turn, our eyes were drawn to a distinct, bright red blood trail along the direction the buck had run. What had appeared to be a clean miss was quickly becoming a promising encounter. With the blood trail profuse and easy to follow, we hadn't traveled 100 yards prior to recovering our buck. Upon further investigation, we discovered the single blade from his broadhead had nicked the buck's jugular vein, leading to a clean and very fortunate kill.

A definition of sacrifice is the offering up of something precious for a cause or a reason. As we study the Old Testament, God gave the Hebrew people a very specific sacrificial system to follow. To make atonement for the sins of the people, this required a blood sacrifice. "For the life of a creature is in the blood, and I have given it to you to make atonement for yourselves on the altar; it is the blood that makes atonement for one's life" (Lev. 17:11). Each time a blood sacrifice was made, the one giving it would have been reminded of the cost of the people's disobedience. Yet the shedding of blood was necessary to cover the scourge and penalty of sin.

As we study Scripture, the entire Old Testament points toward the ultimate sacrifice that was to come—that of Jesus giving His life on our behalf. As Hebrews 9:14 states, "How much more, then, will the blood of Christ, who through the eternal Spirit offered himself unblemished to God, cleanse our consciences from acts that lead to death, so that we may serve the living God!" Jesus came to make the final sacrifice necessary, that of shedding His own blood on the Cross of Calvary. As Jesus stated with His three poignant, dying words, "It is finished" (Jn. 19:30).

Jesus paid the ultimate price that we might have life. His blood made all the difference. As Jesus said of himself, "Greater love has no one than this: to lay down one's life for one's friends" (Jn. 15:13). The Old Testament sacrifices were temporary. Jesus' sacrifice was complete, once and for all, and permanent.

As you study God's Word, you cannot miss Jesus' blood trail. All of Scripture points us toward the Son. His blood offers us salvation, redemption, and forgiveness of sins. He loves us so much He gave His own life that we might live. Won't you accept His free gift today?

F.O.O.L.

The foolish ones took their lamps but
did not take any oil with them.

(MATT. 25:3)

DUSK WAS QUICKLY APPROACHING and it had been a long day of nothing. Dry and hot early season conditions seemed to be contributing to a challenging day of hunting. My brother Doug and I had been covering the miles, attempting different hunting tactics, all to no avail.

With the allure of our beds and a hot meal, we decided to call it a day, committing to resume the chase in the morning. However, just as we began the long trek back to camp, the unmistakable aroma of elk wafted in on the gentle breeze. With the likelihood of game nearby, we agreed to one final calling sequence prior to satisfying our hunger and fatigue.

Moving quickly, Doug positioned himself 60 yards forward as I began a chorus of cow chirps and estrous whines. We agreed to fifteen minutes of calling and if no response, our hike back to the truck would commence.

One of the many challenges you face as an elk hunter is being prepared for the unexpected. You never fully realize when an opportunity might present itself and, unknowingly in our case, a surprise was imminent.

Although I knew my brother's general location, we had lost visual contact. It wasn't until I heard a thump, followed quickly by a frustrated "dog gonnit," that I realized something had gone awry.

As I hurriedly scurried around the brush separating our positions, the scene I witnessed continues to bring tears of laughter to my eyes to this day. Doug, sprawled flat on his back, feet in the air, had fallen backward over a log. He bemoaned that in succumbing to fatigue, he had failed to remain standing for the calling sequence, but instead chose to sit down and rest on a nearby log, feet pointed directly uphill. Even worse, he failed to remove his heavy pack before sitting, and the log he chose as his seat was completely devoid of bark creating a smooth and slick surface.

To his surprise, after only a couple minutes of my cow calling, a 5x5 bull had stealthily emerged from the tree line, a mere 20-yards away. Due to the bull's location directly to his right, it was impossible to turn and draw his bow from his seated position. When he attempted to slowly stand so he could draw without spooking the bull, a "Humpty Dumpty" moment ensued, as the weight of his backpack pulled him backwards, carrying him helplessly downhill over the log. Since that day, my brother has been affectionately known by the camp nickname of F.O.O.L. (Faller Off Of Logs).

To be clear, this humorous acronym doesn't accurately reflect my brother's hunting acumen, as he is one of the more diligent and careful hunters I know. However, in this momentary incident of exhaustion, he was unprepared and it cost him. In Matthew 25, Jesus reminded his listeners to always be ready concerning the coming of His kingdom. Speaking through a parable, Jesus taught of a wedding banquet, describing ten virgins and their oil lamps, but declaring "five of them were foolish and five were wise" (Matt. 25:2). The only distinguishing factor between the two groups was that the wise virgins took oil with them. They were prepared.

The scripture goes on to describe the timing of Jesus's return. Sadly, the foolish virgins were not ready. Verse 10 reads, "But while they were on their way to buy oil, the bridegroom arrived. The virgins who were ready went in with him to the wedding banquet and the door was shut." The foolish virgins had missed their opportunity.

God's desire is that no one is lost. I love the picture in Luke 15 where Jesus is described as the Good Shepherd. Won't He, "leave the ninety-nine others in the wilderness and go to search for the one that is lost until he finds it?" (Luke 15:4) God's love for his children is greater than we can fathom. But He does grant each of us free will and a choice. A choice to choose Jesus or a decision to follow the world. So it begs the question, "Are you ready for Jesus' return?" If not, commit your life to Him today. Make sure you are found to be one of the wise, not one of the unprepared fools!

Shangri-la

I saw the Holy City, the new Jerusalem,
coming down out of heaven from God.

(Rev. 21:2a)

A teacher posed the question, "If you could transport yourself to the most peaceful place on earth, where would that be?" Many of my classmates mentioned places like Hawaii, the beaches of California, or floating their favorite river. Although all of these locations offer some appeal, my mind was instantly transported to a quiet, serene hunting meadow from my childhood. From an early age I was most comfortable and at peace in the woods.

As any outdoorsman can attest, there's something calming about welcoming the morning sunrise, feeling the gentle breeze off a high, alpine meadow, or the calm rustle of leaves flowing through an aspen grove. God's creation, placed before us to explore and experience, continues drawing me back year after year.

With each passing hunting season, I have been fortunate to have had the opportunity to investigate different archery units, both within my home state of Oregon as well as some out-of-state adventures. Each landscape reveals its own unique beauty, whether it be high desert, coastal wetlands, or the peaks of the western mountains. But for all the breathtaking terrain I have covered, there was one specific place, that when first discovered, instantly became a special place in my soul. Elk paradise! A location that has earned the title within our hunting group as simply "Shangri-la."

Websters dictionary defines Shangri-la as, "a remote, beautiful, imaginary place where life approaches perfection."[1] This location matched everything but "imaginary" from that description. Nestled two-thirds down a severe, northwest facing slope, this breathtaking bench offered an excellent feed source, nearby water, ample cover, and gently sloped bedding areas—near perfection for any elk herd to frequent. A gem that is difficult to describe but must only be truly experienced.

It is natural for people to crave places that appeal to their senses of peace and contentment. Many times it seems difficult to get respite from the constant bombardment of negative news in the world around us. From reporting on wars, escalating crime, shootings, or governmental infighting, the internal toll and stress can, at times, feel overwhelming. Yet amidst the chaos we are told in scripture that Jesus already knew these things would happen. Jesus reminded His followers, "In this world you will have trouble. But take heart! I have overcome the world" (Jn. 16:33). Strife and difficulty will not disappear in this life, but we can be confident that Jesus walks beside us through the trials.

Regarding our need for peace and contentment, Jesus also said, "And if I go and prepare a place for you, I will come back and take you to be with me that you also may be where I am" (Jn. 14:3). Jesus is readying a place for us, better than any of us could imagine. We can be encouraged in that, "What no eye has seen, what no ear has heard, and what no human mind has conceived—the things God has prepared for those who love him" (I Cor. 2:9).

Heaven is beyond man's full comprehension. Yet the Bible has given us glimpses of what paradise will look like. From "streets of gold" (Rv. 21:21), to "many rooms" (Jn. 14:2), saints worshipping in "white robes" (Rev. 7:9), to requiring neither "the light of a lamp or the light of the sun, for the Lord God will give them light" (Rev. 22:5). For the believer, this describes our ultimate home.

Jesus has gone and prepared our heavenly "Shangri-la," where life finally reaches perfection. Oh, how I look forward to the day we will finally see our Savior face-to-face.

1. Webster's Third New International, 1993.

The Treacherous Path

Everyone who sins breaks the law; in fact, sin is lawlessness.

(1 JN. 3:4)

WHILE ELK HUNTING THE high country of the western states, maintaining a heightened mental awareness of your surroundings is critical. If not careful and alert, potential pitfalls can derail a hunt in a heartbeat. Factors such as dangerous terrain features or sudden weather changes can pose a real threat. With your mind preoccupied with the prospect of finding elk, it can be easy to get lured into taking a treacherous path.

During a hunt in the mountains of Idaho, we had entered into some prime elk habitat. Fresh game trails abounded and the smell of rutting bulls wafted in the breeze. With a distant bugle echoing from the valley beneath us, our senses were on high alert. In our excitement, what we failed to notice were the collecting storm clouds in the distance.

As we began to make our descent toward the bugling bull below, the once blue skies quickly turned an ominous grey. Hail, thunder, lightning, heavy rains, and fierce winds soon followed as the mountainside turned dangerous. Attempting to make any movement down the steep hillside proved risky. Only after sustaining multiple slips and falls that could have caused severe injury did we make the decision to hunker down and ride out the storm. The risk compared to potential reward was just too great.

While navigating elk habitat there are hourly decisions that are constantly required as to what path to take. Do I ford this river or investigate further downstream for an easier crossing point? Should I scale this rocky outcropping or traverse the longer distance around the ridge? Can I descend this steep chute to the valley below or do I need to locate a safer egress point? As hunters, how we move across the landscape can determine our safety and security in getting back out of the woods in one piece.

Our world presents similar decisions. Temptation seems to lurk around every corner. A person can hardly scan through TV channels, search the internet, or turn on the radio anymore without being constantly enticed by worldly pleasures. Temptations regarding money, possessions, power, or sex are flaunted before us continuously; and sadly, these will always be with us in this world. The question for each of us is, how do we respond? To flirt with sin is a treacherous and dangerous path.

A common excuse you may hear among Christians is their actions only amount to "little sins." A sarcastic remark, some casual gossip, a few swear words, or a quick seductive glance really doesn't hurt anybody, right? The problem is sin never stays little. Like a weed, if unchecked, it spreads and multiplies. Jesus sees our hearts. He warned about not just outward acts of sin but also those committed in your heart. "But I tell you that anyone who looks at a woman lustfully has already committed adultery with her in his heart" (Mt. 5:28).

Let's not tiptoe along the treacherous path of sin, seeing how close we can get prior to succumbing to it. That is just plain foolishness. Instead, let's put on our track shoes and run the other way. Scripture warns us to flee from sin! As Matthew 26:41 implores, "Watch and pray so that you will not fall into temptation. The spirit is willing, but the flesh is weak." The Christian life is not for the passive—we are instructed to reject sinful behavior and proactively grow in holiness. For as Revelation 3:15–16 warns, lukewarm Christianity is not Christianity at all.

Just as a hunter pursues his prey in the wild, may we deliberately and wholeheartedly pursue righteousness in our lives. Let's make it our aim to daily commit to shun evil and pray for victory over temptation. Avoid the treacherous path of sin and follow God's leading for your life this day. Strive to walk in step with the One who has already shown us the way, our Savior Jesus.

When the Forest is Silent

Be still, and know that I am God.

(Ps. 46:10)

It was with great anticipation that my son, Caleb, and I jumped in the truck and headed out on the 900-mile journey to Utah. My brother had unexpectedly drawn a premium elk tag in that coveted state and we couldn't wait to lend a hand.

As with any new hunting season, visions of experiencing multiple animal encounters, hot rutting action, and bugling bulls was at the forefront of our minds. However, on this particular journey, a combination of hot weather, fire smoke, and full moon seemed to have resulted in some "tight-lipped bulls." The forest was silent.

Like any seasoned elk hunter would, we attempted a number of tactics in an effort to elicit a response. Everything from hunting different elevation bands, multiple drainages, not to mention a varied number of calls. Location bugles, challenge bugles, grunts, chuckles, and cow calls, we offered up the full vocal arsenal, only to be left wanting from one ridgetop to the next.

It's the middle of September, why aren't the elk talking? Shouldn't they be responding to our calls? Let's face it, between buying new reeds, bugling practice, listening to numerous hunting podcasts, and covering the miles, we felt as if we had done everything right. Except there was one small exception, the bulls weren't in the mood to talk.

God answers prayer. But sometimes God is silent. As we consider the life of Job, in his pain of losing his crops, livestock, possessions, and most importantly family, he cried out to God looking for answers. For the first 37 chapters of the Book of Job, he asks God for help and relief but is only met with God's silence. It wasn't until chapter 38 that God chose to answer, asking His own question, "Where were you when I laid the earth's foundation? Tell me if you understand" (Jb 38:4). He had heard Job's cries for help but waited to speak. Job was reminded that God answers prayer in His own perfect timing.

How often in life do we try to force our own agenda on the situation? By relying on our own understanding, using our own intellect, or leaning on our ability to fix a problem, we are left disappointed.

God calls us to place our full trust in Him. It may require enduring patience and a place of stillness where we put our human efforts aside. This can be a reminder to "lean not on our own understanding" (Pv. 3:5b) but instead, to find rest and peace in our Savior.

As Christians we are not always going to hear God's voice, but from the example of Job we can learn some practical things to do when God is silent. First, examine your own life. Is there any unconfessed sin? As Psalms 66:18 reads, "If I had cherished sin in my heart, the Lord would not have listened." Second, God's silence can be an opportunity for us to more fully realize His authority over our lives. There is no obligation for God to answer us. Finally, when God is silent, take this time to develop deeper faith. We shouldn't doubt or stop praying. Instead, use this opportunity to press deeper into God and seek Him more diligently.

As you take time to explore the elk woods this season, pause a moment to simply be still before your Creator. Be reminded that God is still present and active. As you await that next bugle, God is present and listening—even when the forest is silent.

Speak Life

Do not let any unwholesome talk come out of your mouths...
(EPH. 4:29A)

THERE ARE MANY IMPORTANT aspects to learning a foreign language. Depending on what is being taught, a new language might require becoming familiar with an entirely new alphabet, use of different sentence structures, or important verbs to ensure accurate conversations. While in high school I took three years of Spanish class. And although learning basic sentences and correct spellings were important, what ultimately separated the students who could converse smoothly and those of us who struggled was in learning correct pronunciation. It was one thing to know how to read and spell the language; it was another thing altogether to get your tongue to cooperate.

As one of the more well-known elk call companies on the market today, Primos has as their company slogan "Speak the Language." The idea being that if a hunter can sound more like an elk, the possibility of success goes up significantly. By mimicking our quarry, it should allow us to get in closer, lure in an inquisitive bull, or sound like an elk herd moving through the woods. Yet becoming proficient with a latex reed in the mouth is easier said than done.

Developing skills required to become a seasoned elk caller takes understanding elk communication, repetition, and practice. Elk talk back and forth to each other in various ways. Having the ability to produce a cow chirp, calf call, bull chuckle, grunt, or full-on bugle can all add up to being a more successful hunter in the woods. There are a multitude of choices in bugle tubes, mouth calls, and even the stretch of latex on a mouth reed. But without proper mouth placement and tongue pressure, you're likely to get a squeaky, off pitch, or ill-timed elk call, alerting the elk to what you really are—human.

Within our hunting party, we will occasionally come across a bull that rightly deserves a nickname. Just like people, bull elk can be distinguished by the language they speak. On this particular hunt, our bull was aptly named the "Whistle Pig" for its high-pitched bugle.

Depending on a bull's mood, a bugle can display emotions such as laziness, courting love, or simply identifying their location to other elk in the area. But when we heard this specific bugle, it sounded like a whistling teapot resonating through the treetops. We had encroached on this bull elk's territory and he was irritated and mad. Before we could even complete a full bugle sequence, Whistle Pig was screaming at full tilt, with the highest pitch, ear-piercing bugle I have ever heard. Try as we might we couldn't replicate that bugle with our mouth reed.

Much the same way, in our daily lives we can generate either a melodious bugle or squeaky response depending on how we use our tongue. Out of our mouths can bring both blessing and life, or curses and death. The tongue holds incredible power. Proverbs 18:21a warns, "The tongue has the power of life and death. . ." It matters what we say.

Our tongues can produce "a gentle answer" (Pv. 15:1a), "overflow of praise" (Ps. 119:171a), and serve as a "tree of life" (Pv. 15:4a). If not careful, however, the tongue can "crush the spirit" (Pv. 15:4b), "stir up anger" (Pv. 15:1b), and can "corrupt the whole body" (Jm 3:6). The Bible goes on to warn that no human can tame the tongue. It is a "restless evil, full of deadly poison" (Jm 3:8). So how can we control what we say?

Pray and ask God for help. For as believers, through the grace of God in our lives we can control our speech. As Philippians 4:13 encourages, "I can do all things through him who gives me strength."

Be intentional in what you say. Let's not be accused of only being hearers of the Word, but let's do what it says. Just as we hope to have the opportunity to season our meat at the end of the hunt, may we also strive to season our speech. As Colossians 4:6a admonishes, "Let your conversation be always full of grace, seasoned with salt. . ." Bring words of encouragement to your spouse, children, or hunting buddy. Commit today to "speak life."

Fear Factor

When I am afraid, I will trust in you

(Ps. 56:3)

As a general rule, whenever I step into the woods for an elk hunt, I go with a hunting partner. Not only for the ease of utilizing a shooter/caller set-up, but also for the camaraderie, company, and safety it brings while hunting in pairs. However, during this particular week, with the hunting starting off slow, the decision was made to split up and do some solo prospecting missions to see if we could turn up some elk.

Prior to the advent of GPS devices, our hunt preparation was relegated to consulting paper maps to determine a general location each of us would investigate. Although I was somewhat familiar with the country before me, there was plenty of uncharted wilderness to be explored. So, with a compass bearing guiding my way, I pushed deep into the backcountry in pursuit of the elusive wapiti.

During any trackless expedition, often the best laid plans take a turn. As I was traversing a high ridgeback, it didn't take long before the alluring sound of a lone bugle resonated from the drainage below. The only problem was this elk's announcement came from the completely opposite direction and 1,500 below where my hunting party expected me to be exploring. If by some unlikely event I became lost or injured, no one would know my location. I was truly alone.

Who, though, can resist the enticement of the call of the wild? Chasing after the king of the forest during the rut, what hunter wouldn't want this opportunity? So without hesitation and with every sense alive, I dove over the ridgetop, going steep and deep in pursuit of my target. For as we often remind each other, if you're not willing to chase a bugle, don't carry an elk call in your pocket.

Descending elevation quickly, it became apparent the bugling was originating from across the opposite canyon face. But as I reached the valley floor, a raging torrent separated my position from the bull, except for one lone fallen log connecting the steep drainage faces. My only way across teetered 15 feet above the creek bottom below.

Throwing caution to the wind, with bow strapped to my backpack, I began slowly shimmying face-first across the divide. It wasn't until I neared the halfway point that reality slapped me squarely in the face. "You dummy! If you fall off this log you're at best breaking something, and at worst not making it out alive!" To compound matters, no one knew of my location.

As fear suddenly gripped every fiber of my being, my body felt momentarily paralyzed as I clung desperately above the rushing waters below. With greatest care, I gingerly began reversing my path. Scooting slowly backwards along the mist-covered log, great relief finally settled over me as my feet touched solid ground. With trembling fear, I vowed then and there to never take such a foolish chance again, particularly while solo hunting in the mountains.

Satan, the enemy of our souls, will often use fear to paralyze believers in an effort to steal our faith. Fear of the future, fear regarding our ability to provide for our daily needs, or simply fear of the unknown are all tactics the devil uses to allow doubt to creep into our thoughts. As we attempt to forecast what the future may hold, it often seems cloudy and uncertain. By allowing fear and anxiety to grow, we grant our enemy influence over our lives.

So, how do we wrench back control of our fears and allow God to take the reins of our lives? In Psalms 56:3, David says, "When I am afraid, I will trust in you." Likewise, in Deuteronomy 31:6 the Bible encourages the believer to, "Be strong and courageous. Do not be afraid or terrified because of them, for the Lord your God goes with you; he will never leave you nor forsake you." It's a simple yet profound truth. We must yield control and place our trust fully in the Lord.

While on this earth, the scripture teaches that we have a real and clear enemy—the devil. But knowing your adversary is only half the battle. Overcoming fear through trust in our Heavenly Father is our battleplan. As the Psalmist wrote, "Even though I walk through the valley of the shadow of death, I will fear no evil, for you are with me. . ." (Ps. 23:4).

So, the next time you feel fear overtaking your thoughts, turn your focus to the Savior. May we not go only halfway but rather traverse the divide, not allowing the enemy to gain a foothold in our lives. Place your unwavering faith in an all-powerful God for He is trustworthy!

Soul Recharge

He makes me lie down in green pastures, he leads
me beside quiet waters, he refreshes my soul.

(Ps. 23:2–3a)

WHEN TAKING A TRIP, isn't it nice sometimes to just get off the interstate and take the backcountry roads, even if it takes a little longer to arrive at your destination? My dad was notorious for this, avoiding traffic at all costs. During one summer just for fun, he went so far as to attempt to drive west to east, across the entire width of our home state of Oregon, without ever touching pavement. My dad certainly instilled in me that same desire to take the road less traveled. A line out of Robert Frost's poem, "The Road Not Taken" resonates as it reads, "Two roads diverged in a wood, and I—I took the one less traveled by, and that has made all the difference."[1]

One of the beauties of hunting is that it allows us a brief respite from the hustle and bustle of daily life. A chance to get away from buildings, concrete, and traffic congestion to simply soak in God's creation. I realize not every reader resides in an urban environment. But I think we all would agree that periodically disconnecting from some of the pressures of our weekly routine is necessary and refreshing. We all could benefit from a "soul recharge" that only the outdoors can provide.

1. Frost et al., *Road Not Taken.*

I am predominantly an archery hunter. Nationwide statistics reveal that only about 10% of archers fill their elk tags each year. Although I've experienced a little better success than the average, as many would agree, elk hunting is just plain hard. I've always said, if your primary goal with hunting is to put meat in the freezer, I might recommend digging out the rifle. But the allure and draw of September beauty in the mountains during archery season for me is unmatched.

From the dawn of creation, the heavens have declared God's creation. As announced in Psalm 96:11–12, "Let the heavens rejoice, let the earth be glad; let the sea resound, and all that is in it. Let the fields be jubilant, and everything in them; let all the trees of the forest sing for joy." Pause a moment and take a look around at God's handiwork. Those high alpine meadows, rustling aspen groves, secluded brooks, or majestic forest stands—the evidence is right before each of us. Don't miss it.

God displays His glory and creativity all around us where much can be learned if we simply slow down and recognize His creation. As you step from rock to rock across the next stream bed, may it prompt you to remember God's reliability as we read, "There is no one holy like the Lord; there is no one besides you; there is no Rock like our God" (I Sam. 2:2). Or as you gaze across the next colorful meadow be reminded of God's design as Luke 12:27 reminds, "Consider how the wild flowers grow. They do not labor or spin. Yet I tell you, not even Soloman in all his splendor was dressed like one of these." Or as you lie down at night and gaze up into the endless galaxies of the sky, be in awe of God's infinite power as Psalm 8:3 reads, "When I consider your heavens, the work of your fingers, the moon and the stars, which you have set in place. . ."

Wherever you are hunting this season, take time to pause and breathe in God's presence. Some of you may be reading this as you sit on a whitetail deer stand in the Midwest, others as you rest following a steep climb up craggy cliffs in pursuit of big horn sheep. Some readers may be hearing these words as you sit and wait inside a blind for migrating winter duck or geese to appear. Or finally others may read them while elk hunting with either bow or rifle in hand, pursuing what I consider to be North America's most majestic big game animal. Take a moment to look around. Pause for a moment and simply listen to the sound of nature. Allow the God of the universe to refresh your spirit as you receive a "soul recharge" this day.

Unashamedly Run!

Let us run with perseverance the race marked our for us

(HEB. 12:1)

IT WAS 3 P.M. in the afternoon and we had just arrived at a brand new hunting spot. We weren't sure what to expect but the anticipation level was at an all-time high. As we had driven in earlier that day, meat quarters were hanging in several camps, only adding to the excitement.

Once camp was set up, my hunting buddy Ron, brother Doug, and I decided to take a quick motorcycle ride to help get a lay of the land. Our plan was to cover a few miles and spend some time glassing various vantage points to help determine our initial hunt plan for the week. However, before we had even ridden a minute from camp, a 5-point bull elk suddenly ran across the road, narrowly missing Ron's front tire. As fast as possible, we scrambled back to camp, grabbed our hunting gear, and dove off into the woods chasing that bull.

Doug and I decided to try a team bugling tactic while Ron would cover other ground with a spot and stalk technique, hoping to turn up the bull again. It didn't take long before Doug's bugle elicited an agitated response from the bull and the game was on. In an effort to be aggressive, anytime the bull would answer our call we would immediately run through the woods, straight at the bugling sound, attempting to present a challenge. Call, response, run!

Within minutes, we had closed the distance and the bull was coming unglued. Doug sent out one more challenge bugle and the 5-point emerged, coming our way. Having already positioned myself ahead of the caller, I was set up in an ideal position for a shot. Before I could think, the bull turned broadside and I drew, settled my 40-yd. pin, and watched as my arrow landed true. My first branch antler bull down, all because we ran!

In Hebrews, the writer likens the Christian experience to a race, where it reads, ". . .let us throw off everything that hinders and the sin that so easily entangles. And let us run with perseverance the race marked out for us" (Heb. 12:1). During my youth I participated in several different sports. I learned at an early age that if you wish to be successful in athletics it takes discipline.

Likewise, we need to take the same deliberate and focused approach to our Christian life. The apostle Paul admonishes his readers, "Everyone who competes in the games goes into strict training. . .we do it to get a crown that will last forever" (1 Cor. 9:25). In other words, don't take your relationship with God lightly. We must be as serious with training our faith as we would be in training for a competition.

We are also reminded in scripture that we don't have to run this race alone. Isaiah 40:31 encourages, "but those who hope in the Lord will renew their strength. They will soar on wings like eagles; they will run and not grow weary, they will walk and not be faint." God will supply each of us the strength and stamina we need to finish the race.

Life presents daily challenges, struggles, and obstacles that can divert our attention away from Christ. But be reminded that we follow the "author and perfector of our faith" (Heb. 12:2a). He will not leave us as orphans. Jesus has already faced it all and won the race. So let's unashamedly run towards our Creator and hold nothing back.

True North Slope

*Come to me, all you who are weary and
burdened, and I will give you rest.*

(MATT. 11:28)

WHEN I FIRST STARTED archery hunting as a youth, to say I had a
plan for a given day in terms of where to go, terrain features to look
for, or understanding the specific behaviors of the animals I was
chasing would have been a stretch. My initial hunt plan consisted
of getting dropped off along a stretch of a road, setting a compass
bearing back to camp, and wandering through the woods, hoping
to jump some game. Little care went into intently studying maps
or understanding elk habits to improve my success. As you might
have guessed, the success rate in filling my tag was poor.

Over the years, with time spent in the woods and possessing
a better understanding of elk behavior, I have learned a few things
in terms of targeting animals. Learning how to read sign, appre-
ciating elk habits of where they like to feed, bed, and water, and
the e-scouting technologies available to today's hunter, have all
advanced my knowledge tremendously. In recent years, one of the
most prominent features I use for locating elk is placing particular
focus on north-facing slopes.

Staying cool on a hot day can be just as taxing on an elk as
staying warm in the middle of winter. Given that elk are walking
around with essentially a large fur coat on, accessing an area to
cool themselves during the hot daytime hours of late summer is

necessary. As many hunters who have chased elk in August or September have come to realize, a predominantly north-facing slope can offer this place of rest and solitude. Also, due in large part to a decreased amount of heat and sunlight, north slopes are often more heavily wooded and brushy.

All these factors create a perfect environment for elk to gravitate toward during mid-day. North slopes provide a cool place to rest, dense cover for protection, increased likelihood of water nearby, and security from approaching predators.

As I have hunted a multitude of different mountain ranges in the west, I have come to appreciate the vast changes in the landscape. As the hunter drops over from one side of the mountain to the other, you can virtually feel the change in climate and ecology. The same is true when entering into a walk with Jesus. Jesus is our true north slope!

More than ever, when I watch the news, I see a world filled with chaos, confusion, conflict, and uncertainty. But thanks be to God, He offers us rest within the mess. In Phillipians 4:7, it reads "And the peace of God, which transcends all understanding, will guard your hearts and your minds in Christ Jesus." We can rest in knowing that God is watching over us.

Becoming a follower of Christ does not eliminate trouble coming your way. In fact, Jesus warned His disciples that persecution should be expected. John 16:33 states, "In this world you will have trouble. But take heart! I have overcome the world."

Rest, solitude, refreshment, protection. God offers this to each of us today. Amidst the chaos of life, Jesus reminds us that He has already overcome. Trust in Jesus and allow His promises and presence to be your true north slope today.

Vantage Point

*The eyes of the Lord are everywhere, keeping
watch on the wicked and the good.*

(Prov. 15:3)

I must admit, I've been accused of not being the most patient person in the world. Particularly as it relates to elk hunting my M.O. is geared towards investigating what's over the next rise, around the bend, or across the creek. In case you hadn't guessed, I have a tough time sitting still.

Now don't get me wrong, when I find an open glassing point and have an opportunity to cover country with my binoculars versus boots, I take full advantage. The only difference is usually my hunting partner is just getting comfortable and settling in with their glass when I'm ready to roll. After a quick scan of the adjacent hillside if nothing jumps out, it's time to cover more country.

But as I have gotten older and hopefully a little wiser, I have come to better appreciate all the different methods of finding game. As my hunting partners have demonstrated, there are distinct advantages to simply slowing down and using the benefits of a good vantage point.

Taking in country from a distance can provide a unique perspective. A rock outcropping here, a finger ridge of trees there, or a bench nestled along a steep canyon face that if viewed up close might not be fully appreciated. More importantly as a hunter, the ability to locate game from a distance without having to put miles on your boots has proven to be a valuable saver of both time and energy. Somewhat reluctantly, I have begun to spend extra time behind the glass. It takes patience but it's amazing what can be revealed by just gaining a view from above.

It's tempting to view our world through the daily lens of life circumstances. I've been as guilty as anyone about forgetting the big picture and why I've been placed on this earth to begin with. Were we created to simply work, raise a family, do a few good deeds toward our fellow man and die? There has to be more to life than that.

God has a different vantage point. For the Bible teaches, "all things were created through him and for him" (Col. 1:16b). You see, each one of us has been uniquely created for a purpose. God doesn't make mistakes. As King David articulated, "I praise you because I am fearfully and wonderfully made" (Ps. 139:14a). God knows you so well, scripture teaches, "even the very hairs of your head are all numbered" (Matt. 10:30).

Isn't it comforting to realize you are known and loved by the Creator of the universe? Our God, greater and mightier than the human mind can fathom, cares personally about you and me. A God who describes himself in Revelation this way, "I am the Alpha and the Omega, says the Lord God, 'who is, and who was, and who is to come, the Almighty" (Rev. 1:8).

May we catch a glimpse of God's vantage point today. A God who sees our past, leads our present, and holds our future in His hands. A Savior who promises to never leave us or forsake us.

Be reminded that you are God's special creation and there is no one like you. You were created for a purpose. Strive this day to view your life from God's vantage point and go walk in the fullness of His love for you today.

A Father's Love

*If you, then, though you are evil, know how to give good
gifts to your children, how much more will your Father
in heaven give good gifts to those who ask him!*

(MT. 7:11)

FOR THOSE OF YOU who have kids, do you remember the emotion when your children were born? The excitement and anticipation of what this new bundle of life had in store? As new parents, my wife, Michele, and I didn't fully realize what we were getting ourselves into. At times we felt as if we were flying by the "seat of our pants" while attempting to figure out this whole parenting thing. And although I'm certain we made plenty of mistakes along the way, the one thing I can state with certainty is that there was, and always will remain, a deep, unconditional love for each of our three children.

There was nothing we wouldn't do for those three little rugrats. Don't get me wrong. There were days that would try our patience, turn a few hairs grey, or cause us to pull out a couple hairs altogether. But I can say with confidence we have enjoyed every step of the journey. From experiencing a first word or first tooth lost as young kids, onto their first shave, first date, or first time driving, the milestones and memories are priceless.

As a dad who loves the outdoors, I felt particularly blessed to have had the opportunity to raise three boys that shared my enthusiasm. From motorcycle riding, backcountry hiking trips, fishing floats, or playing every outdoor sport imaginable, the adventures were endless. Although each outing together held special meaning, there is something extra special for a father when you witness your children having hunting success.

I have been fortunate to have witnessed all three of my boys harvest an animal. Celebrating in the success with Caleb after arrowing his first bull. Or getting to experience a double-blessing over Labor Day weekend, as both Kyle and Lucas on consecutive days, saw their bullets strike true. Packing out two elk on back-to-back days is definitely a labor of love, rejoicing with both Kyle and Lucas as they punched their first elk tags. I must say, having an opportunity to be a part of my boy's successes brought a special joy, one that is experienced only through a father's heart.

You see, there was an interesting pivot that occurred within my own psyche as to the primary focus when stepping into the elk woods. As my family would attest, I am a die-hard hunter to the core. However, as my three boys grew older, I noticed my hunting priorities shifting from myself and my own personal success to that of my kids. If I could also fill my tag in the process, all the better. But a father's love, wanting the best for my children's success, took precedence.

When I sit back and contemplate the verse that reads, "If you, then, though you are evil, know how to give good gifts to your children, how much more will your Father in heaven give good gifts to those who ask him!" (Mt. 7:11) I am awestruck at how incredible God's love is for us. For in my own humanity, I know how desperately I love my kids. I would lay down my very life for my family as would most fathers. But God's love doesn't stop there. For in Romans 5:7–8 we read, "Very rarely will anyone die for a righteous person. . .But God demonstrates his own love for us in this: While we were still sinners, Christ died for us."

You see, God doesn't only love us, but He has adopted us into His family. We are His sons and daughters. 1 John 3:1a reads, "See what great love the Father has lavished on us, that we should be called children of God!"

He knows you personally. The Scripture says he calls you by name. You are precious to God in that He will leave the entire flock to pursue you, as the Bible reads, ". . .will he not leave the ninety-nine on the hills and go to look for the one who wandered off?" (Mt. 18:12).

I pray you are reminded how deep and wide and long your Heavenly Father's love is for you today. No matter how far you may have strayed, God is constantly pursuing you and stands with His arms open wide, ready to welcome each of us. Our Father says about himself, "Here I am! I stand at the door and knock. If anyone hears my voice and opens the door, I will come in and eat with that person, and they with me." (Rev. 3:20).

God loves you unconditionally. He wishes to lavish on each of us the good gifts of His presence. Receive the Father's love for you today!

Perfume Station

For we are to God the pleasing aroma of Christ...

(2 Cor. 2:15)

On this particular week the hunting had been hot and dry, causing moving around in the woods to be difficult. Each step sounded like popcorn, so the prospects of sneaking up on any game was low.

If I had my preference, calling in bulls during September cannot be matched. The excitement and energy that comes along with a bull screaming full-force, looking for a fight, gets any elk hunter's blood boiling.

Anyone that knows me well would attest that I have a tough time sitting still. The idea of sitting on a tree stand without moving for hours on end is like pulling teeth. However, given the dry conditions on this day, I relented and decided to hike the four miles into a tree stand we had erected earlier in the season, overlooking a secluded wallow.

Mature bull elk use scent to both attract their mates and display dominance. So, aside from being a place to cool down, a wallow can act like a perfume station. Using the water and mud mixed with their own bodily odors, a wallow can exponentially add to an elk's ability to spread their scent.

Fortunately for me and my lack of patience, I hadn't been in the tree stand for more than 30 minutes when four elk appeared through the nearby trees. As they made their way slowly toward the wallow, I knew my chance was now. On this day it was a steady 30-yard shot that tracked true, hitting its mark. Elk down! A visit to the perfume station had paid off!

As I contemplate the use of a wallow for elk, it reminds me that the lives we live, the words we use, and the actions we take bring about their own aroma. God calls us to produce a pleasing aroma, one that attracts others to Christ. We are reminded that Jesus, "has committed to us the message of reconciliation. We are therefore Christ's ambassadors" (2 Cor. 5:19–20a).

As believers, just as Jesus commissioned his disciples to ". . .go and make disciples of all nations. . ." (Mt. 28:19a), we too are to be His witnesses to the world around us. We are blessed with the opportunity to be the hands and feet of Jesus to the world in which we live. As Philippians 2:3–4 reminds us, ". . .in humility value others above yourselves, not looking to your own interests but each of you to the interests of the others." May others be attracted to God through his Holy Spirit living in each of us.

I must admit, I have acted in ways that have surely soured others. The scent trail was a stenchy one, produced by my own sin, selfishness, and pride. Thank God He has made a way for you and me. We don't have to try and concoct a pleasing aroma through our own efforts but instead, God's Spirit creates in us what we were helpless to do for ourselves. Allow yourself to wallow in God's amazing love and gifts, so we all might become a holy "perfume station", serving as an attractant to those around us.

Velociraptor Experience

My sheep listen to my voice; I know them, and they follow me.
(Jn. 10:27)

From my vantage standing atop an elevated stump, brush was swaying side-to-side, ear tops and antler tips rose above the fray, and a bugle frenzy had ensued. Our elk hunt had suddenly been thrown into confusion and chaos!

There are numerous methods to try and locate elk. Identifying well-used travel corridors, freshly made bull rubs, or searching out promising bedding areas are all options to employ. However, one of our more successful strategies, especially when the elk calling slows down, is to utilize locator bugles at nighttime. Often when the elk are "call shy" during the day, you can still elicit a response after dark. A different voice at a different time can, at times, make all the difference.

The night prior after casting out several bugles in the dark, our hunting party was able to pinpoint a bull at the bottom of a steep drainage. With our hunt plan identified, we proceeded to drop 1,500 feet through the awakening dawn, positioning ourselves just downwind of our target bull at first light. It didn't take long after issuing our first call of the morning that we received a challenge response back. The bull was right where we had left him the night before!

Positioned downhill and downwind of the bull at first light, we hoped to quickly coax him into shooting range. Unfortunately, the bull had other plans as he proceeded to round up his herd and began heading in the opposite direction back uphill. He had worked hard in building his breeding harem of cows and he wasn't about to let an intruder bull in on the action.

So stiffening our resolve, we began dogging our bull back to the top of the ridge. We would bugle and move toward the bull, the bull would respond and move away, and so it went as we continued to pursue him up the ridge. Although timber separated our view, anticipation began to mount as we realized we were gradually closing the distance.

Unbeknownst to us, at the top of the ridge was a thicket of head-high manzanita bushes, and the elk herd had selected that thicket as a place to stop and congregate. What we encountered as we crested the ridgetop will forever be brandished in our memories. Akin to a scene straight out of *Jurassic Park* when the cow is lowered into the velociraptor enclosure and all that can be seen is the swaying of branches as it is devoured, so it was inside the manzanita grove. With the elk herd suddenly dispersed and our bugling continuing at a torrid pace, the herd bull was sent into a frenzy and all we could see was the rustling of brush as elk moved around us in all directions. All method of elk talk ensued—cow chirps, lost calf calls, and non-stop bugling action as the herd attempted to locate one another, with us standing right in the middle of the action! Within mere feet of our location, brush swayed and elk called back and forth from every direction, resulting in a hunt that we now simply refer to as "The Velociraptor Experience."

Just as our herd bull had become confused and irritated with the multitude of elk calls ringing in his ears, it can often be difficult to know which voice to listen to in our own lives. We are constantly bombarded by a plethora of opinions. Whether it be news outlets, politicians, social media, or our own circle of influence of family and friends, there can often be a lot of voices playing in our head. How do we make wise decisions?

It starts with knowing God. John 8:47 simply yet profoundly states, "Whoever belongs to God hears what God says. The reason you do not hear is that you do not belong to God." How can we expect to wade through the confusion this world offers if we're not standing on the solid foundation of God's word? I love Jesus' promise that if we pursue Him, He will meet us where we are. As the prophet Jeremiah wrote, "You will seek me and find me when you seek me with all your heart" (Jer. 29:13).

If there is anything certain in life beyond death and taxes, it's that our circumstances will never remain the same. Psalms 46:6 reminds us, "Nations are in uproar, kingdoms fall. . ." Yet the passage goes on to encourage that, "The Lord Almighty is with us; the God of Jacob is our fortress" (Ps. 46:7). God is our refuge above the noise.

My prayer for you today is that you might desire to know Jesus more deeply. Choose the wisdom that God offers through the Bible. Pattern your life after the wise man who built his life on the solid foundation of God's Word. As we are reminded in Matthew 7:24, "Therefore everyone who hears these words of mine and puts them into practice is like a wise man who built his house on the rock."

Place your feet firmly on the solid rock of God's Word. Rulers, entertainers, and social influencers of this world will come and go but the Word of God will last forever. Don't allow the "shifting bushes" and confusion of outside voices to dominate your thinking but instead, turn your ear to the voice of the Almighty. Read His word, trust in His promises for your life, and be reminded that our God will never change.

Two Steps Closer

I have considered my ways and have
turned my steps to your statutes.

(Ps. 119:59)

How often in hunting do we hear the story, "If I could have snuck in just a little bit closer, I could have gotten the shot"? The ability to close the distance on our quarry improves our odds for success. A few more steps around a bush, a quiet crawl over a log, or a silent slip up to the next tree can all be efforts to give ourselves a more desirable shot.

On this particular morning, it was nearing the end of our week-long hunt and my good buddy Les, relatively new to the sport of archery, had not had many animal encounters during the trip. Given it was the last day of our hunt, myself and a couple others from our group, decided to join Les for one final foray through the woods to see if we could turn up some elk or deer and give him an opportunity to fill a tag.

As we entered some prime-looking habitat, we hadn't gone far before a nice, symmetrical 3-pt. mule deer stood up from his bed and froze. Being the good guides that we were, my brother quickly ranged the animal at 51 yards and whispered the distance into Les's ear. However, realizing this distance was on the outer limits of his comfortable shooting range, Les thought about the shot briefly but quickly discounted it. Upon hearing the yardage, Les whispered back, "That shot is much too far. I need to get closer."

Before we could respond, Les suddenly took two quick steps toward the deer, drew, and launched his arrow. Unfortunately, we witnessed the arrow glide harmlessly into the bushes at the buck's feet. As we watched the buck bound gracefully over the ridge, my brother proceeded to announce the new and improved distance of "49 yards." We couldn't help but laugh all the way back to camp at how a 51-yard shot was too long, but 49 yards made all the difference!

As I have grown in my faith, I have learned that the Christian experience is definitely a journey, not a destination. As we take determined steps to move closer to Jesus, God is faithful to reveal himself to us in new ways along the journey.

It was once said to me, based on the daily decisions you make, you choose to either take a step closer or a step farther away from Jesus. Just as the Psalmist determined, "I have considered my ways and have turned my step to your statutes." (Ps. 119:59), my same desire is to continue to press into Jesus. My aim is to make each decision in my life one that will result in drawing me closer to God.

Today, I challenge you to make a conscious decision to grow deeper in your faith. Allow yourself to be guided by the Almighty. Unlike the buck that disappeared over the ridge, God will not flee from you. Instead, as is promised in James 4:8, when you "draw near to God, He will draw near to you." Commit to take one or *two steps closer* to Him today and watch what happens.

Light In, Heavy Out

Run with perseverance the race marked out for us.

(HEB. 12:1B)

OVER THE YEARS I'VE done my share of hard work. Growing up in a rural setting in Oregon with two parents who were born and bred in the heart of the Midwest, a strong work ethic was instilled in both myself and my siblings from an early age. Aside from normal chores around the house, as I grew older I held summer jobs ranging from working as a farm laborer, timber cutter, lumber yardman, appliance deliveryman, and Alaska fisherman, all before the age of 21. I've always figured a little blood and sweat is good for the soul.

I guess you could say I approach elk hunting with a similar mentality. If you work hard, put in the time and cover the miles, good things usually happen. And even if you're not successful, you can at least feel confident that you gave it an honest effort.

On this particular hunt, our party was at the 10-day mark, having already traversed over 100 miles of hiking and thousands of feet of elevation during elk hunts in both Utah and Idaho. We were covering ample country but up until this point were coming up empty handed. To say the least, this 55-year-old man's legs were feeling the fatigue factor.

But as the saying goes, it only takes finding the one elk that wants to be vocal that day. My son Caleb and I were fortunate enough during an evening hunt to get an interested bull answering our cow calls. As I attempted to keep the bull's attention, Caleb quietly closed the distance.

Noting there was only a small window in which he could place an arrow, Caleb waited patiently for an opportunity to present itself. With the bull getting more fired up by the minute yet with sunset quickly approaching, he would have to close the deal soon. Fortunately, following another series of cow calls, we were able to coax our quarry out to where his vitals were momentarily exposed, blessing Caleb with a slam dunk 25-yard shot on a beautiful 5x5 bull! Our persistence had paid off. But as any hunter would attest, once you put an animal on the ground, the real work begins.

After locating the bull and reconnecting with our hunting party, we collectively strapped on our pack frames and with rope and knife in hand, started the 4-mile journey back to retrieve Caleb's bull. Although this process requires a lot of work, the joy of finally filling a tag and supplying your home with meat for the next year is truly satisfying.

By early the next morning, we had the elk quartered up with pack frames loaded. But as we assessed our route back to camp, we quickly realized this was going to be more challenging than expected.

Up and down ridges, clearing logs, wading through brush, all are much more challenging with an extra 80 lbs. strapped to your back. The desire was strong to stop and give up. But with each step we took, the thought of camp and completion of the task weighed heavily on our minds. As we rounded the final bend and with our destination in sight, we realized all our hard work had paid off. Light in, heavy out was complete.

Much like the challenge of hard work or a heavy pack out, our Christian walk can present obstacles to overcome as well. The temptations of this world can often be alluring, offering an easier route and distracting us from our ultimate goal. However, in Hebrews 12, the author encourages us to "run with perseverance the race marked out for us." The word "perseverance" can be likened to a struggle and the hard work and tenacity needed to overcome it.

The Christian life is not promised to be easy. In fact, Jesus admonished His followers that "Whoever wants to be my disciple must deny themselves and take up their cross daily and follow me." (Luke 14:26) Walking in faith will require sacrifice, focus, and persistence. But remember, God is faithful and He has promised to give us "everything we need for a godly life" (2 Pet. 1:3).

So press into Jesus, don't give up, and commit each day to persevere. Be willing to make the necessary sacrifices and do the hard work required in following God's commands. For the prize that awaits is worth every step.

Valley of Death

*Even though I walk through the valley of the shadow
of death, I will fear no evil, for you are with me. . .*
(Ps. 23:4a ESV)

There's no greater thrill than a mountaintop experience—
both literally and figuratively. Something about reaching the
summit of a mountain is simply exhilarating. To be successful it
requires strategy in determining your route, bringing along the
proper essentials, and physical preparation prior to the climb.
When accomplished, unique feelings of satisfaction and joy soon
follow. You want to unabashedly throw your hands in the air in
celebration!

In the same way, we all long for victorious or "mountaintop
experiences" in our everyday lives. No one strives to fail. Just look
at your friends' social media posts. People celebrate all types of ac-
complishments—new relationships, job promotions, graduations,
or hunting conquests—these are the stories we wish to share. Con-
versely, there is a glaring absence of posts regarding disappointments and dark days. There is no celebration in the valley.

It takes a certain level of courage for anyone to enter into the
wild chasing elk. I applaud each and every hunter who makes the
attempt. For you see, elk hunting, approached properly, requires
sacrifice. Whether it be sleep, energy expended, time away from
family, or dangers encountered in the woods, there is a cost. One
definition of a coward includes, "a person who lacks the courage to

do or endure dangerous or unpleasant things."[1] So as elk hunters, I hold in high esteem each one who has the courage to try.

At times, it seems the line between stupidity and courage can become blurred. In one poignant example, my brother and I decided to drop steep and deep into a backcountry basin we knew held elk. The secluded valley was over 3 miles from the trailhead and the trailhead was a 45-minute drive from camp, so in order to be in prime position at first light we decided to hike in the day before and spend the night on the ground with nothing but a light sleeping bag as protection against the elements. During the daylight hours, this valley floor is an elk hunter's paradise. Lush meadows, a burbling stream, nearby benches, and towering rock faces combine to make this destination worth the effort. Yet as the sun disappeared behind the ridge and darkness fell, this beautiful looking valley turned dangerous.

As my brother and I wriggled into our sleeping bags for the night, we soon became aware of the deadly cold that awaited. As the hours passed, without either sleeping pad or tent for protection, the temperature on the valley floor turned subzero. Descending temperature on this clear September night along with an icy stream flowing nearby that literally sucked the warmth from the air combined to make our temporary bed an icebox. With the extreme cold and our constant shivering, sleep was out of the question. All we could do was bury our heads in our all-too-thin sleeping bags and wait for dawn. In an effort to place ourselves near a prime elk feeding area at first light, we nearly froze ourselves to death!

No one is immune from walking through valleys in their lives. In fact, James 1:2 reminds us that we will all face challenges when it states, "Consider it pure joy, my brothers and sisters, whenever you face trials of many kinds. . ." The comfort for the believer is that we never have to walk alone. "So do not fear, for I am with you; do not be dismayed, for I am your God" (Is. 41:10). Better yet, God promises to go before us into battle. Deuteronomy 20:4 encourages, "For the Lord your God is the one who goes with

1. Webster's Third New International, 1993.

you to fight for you against your enemies to give you victory." God provides the Christian with uncommon courage.

So, whatever valley you are walking through today, have full confidence that God goes before you. He promises, "I will not leave you as orphans; I will come to you" (Jn. 14:18). He will also equip you properly to meet any challenge you are facing. Unlike our sleeping experience where we didn't pack enough warm equipment, God has supplied each believer with His full armor. Be encouraged today that you don't fight your battles alone. Place renewed trust in our Savior today. He has already won.

Center Punch

*For the word of God is alive and active. Sharper
than any double-edged sword, it penetrates even
to dividing soul and spirit, joints and marrow; it
judges the thoughts and attitudes of the heart.*

(Heb. 4:12)

Didn't things always seem larger than life when you were
younger? That plate of food you could never finish. Those endless
hallways in your grade school. Or that tree in the backyard that
seemed much too high to climb.

As a child, the perspective we have of the world around us
can often be skewed from the actual truth. Everything is new, different, and exciting as we encounter new realities and experiences.
So it was for my youngest son Lucas as he embarked on his first
deer hunt.

After spending many seasons in elk hunting camp watching
his grandpa, dad, older brothers, and extended family bring meat
back to camp, it was finally Lucas's turn to carry a tag in his pocket.
With hunter's safety class completed and plenty of archery practice
at home, the anticipation of finally getting his own opportunity to
hunt game was almost too much to contain.

Following a few days of scouting, we identified a travel pattern that a couple young bucks seemed to prefer. Setting up near a
small meadow, it didn't take long before a nice, forked-horn mule

deer emerged from the adjacent viny maple thicket. Lucas could barely hold back his excitement as the deer's vitals came into view.

With trembling hands, he carefully drew back his 40 lb. Hoyt compound bow and took aim. Shot, impact, and priceless reaction. Mimicking a humorous saying from the legendary whitetail hunter Stan Potts, Lucas turned to me and exclaimed, "I smoked him! I center punched him!" Unfortunately, his young mind's perspective didn't quite meet reality.

For as we watched the buck quickly scamper away, blood was trailing down the back hind quarter instead of the vitals. What Lucas thought was a "center punch" instead became a long blood trail to follow.

For every hunter that steps into the woods, whether it be with rifle or archery equipment, the potential of wounding an animal is always a concern. You do your best to ready yourself, be practiced up, and place yourself in optimal position for a clean shot, but as most hunters know, things just happen. An unseen limb, a miscalculation of distance, a jerk of the hand. So many factors must be right to make a clean kill.

Fortunately, in this case, we were able to successfully track the deer with Lucas placing a final kill shot on his first buck. Ultimately, a fatal shot with the final arrow left in his quiver landed true. But as we know, our hunting stories don't always end so successfully.

When following God, our expectations of the Christian life don't always align with God's word. Particularly as a new believer, my understanding was that once I became a Christian my life would be easy. However, scripture reminds us, "do not be surprised at the fiery ordeal that has come on you. . .But rejoice inasmuch as you participate in the sufferings of Christ." (1 Pet. 4:12–13). Additionally, Jesus reminded His disciples that, "In this world you will have trouble. But take heart! I have overcome the world" (Jn. 16:33).

Misconceptions held about God and the Christian life can hinder our growth and maturity in the faith. One example is believing all Christians are loving, perfect people. Yet the book of Colossians urges us to "Forgive as the Lord forgave you" (Col. 3:13). None of us is perfect and all are in need of forgiveness. Another misconception is that bad things don't happen to truly godly people. Yet we see the Apostle Paul shipwrecked, the disciples martyred, and Jesus ultimately crucified.

The Scripture is our ultimate truth. God has provided us direct access to Him through His Word. We are reminded that, "All Scripture is God-breathed. . ." (2 Tim. 3:16). The words we read may, at times, be hard to hear. But I encourage you to allow God's truth to penetrate your life today. "For the word of God is alive and active. Sharper than any double-edged sword. . ." (Heb. 4:12a).

As we seek to grow deeper in our faith, allow God's Word to "center punch" your soul today. For the Bible is truth. You can trust Him. Gain God's perspective through His Word today.

Thief of the Woods

The thief comes only to steal and kill and destroy; I have come that they may have life, and have it to the full.

(Jn. 10:10)

THE AIR WAS CRISP with fall colors turning and with the elk rut in full swing, making for ideal conditions on this September morning. As my son, Caleb, and I dropped into one of our favorite canyons, our minds were brimming with confidence.

Within minutes of our descent into the orange and yellow clad drainage, a singular bugle rose from the mist-covered valley below. The hunt was on!

In an effort to close the distance, we stealthily moved our way down the mountain, taking care to follow game trails and use cover to hide our approach. The further we moved, the closer the bugling became, confirming to us that we had not yet disturbed our bull.

Once at the proper elevation and with the wind in our favor, Caleb positioned himself 80 yards ahead as I began a final calling sequence. The bull continued his intense bugling, immediately answering my calls while moving closer to our location with every response. The setup was working!

However, as quickly as the calling had escalated the forest went silent. What had been working up to that point now unexpectedly had no effect. We were shocked and bewildered as to what could have gone wrong as we were confident that the bull couldn't see, hear, or smell us from our present location.

Suddenly, without warning, the brush between ourselves and the elk began to rustle. Within seconds a mature grey wolf emerged and stood broadside a mere 60 yards away, offering us a momentary glimpse. As quickly as the wolf appeared it was gone, slipping away into the landscape and scaring our bull away with it. The thief of the woods had stolen our opportunity.

In John 10, as Jesus was speaking to the Pharisees, He described the relationship He would have with His children. Jesus likened himself to a shepherd and offered an example to His listeners of how, just like sheep know their master's voice, we too can know and recognize the voice of God. However, within the same teaching, we are cautioned to be aware of the thief that wishes to "steal and kill and destroy" (Jn. 10:10).

Satan is real. He wants nothing more than to distract, divert, and redirect our allegiances away from the one true God. Don't let him! Avoid giving the devil a foothold in your life. The devil is described as your enemy that "prowls around like a roaring lion looking for someone to devour" (1 Pet. 5:8b). He's looking for that chink in your armor, a weakness he can take advantage of.

Stand guard, stay alert, remain in God's word. Just like the wolf stole our chance at a bugling bull, don't allow the "thief of our souls" to steal your reward.

Bull with a Bugle Tube

My sheep listen to my voice; I know them, and they follow me.
(Jn. 10:27)

WHEN YOU LOOK AT the hunting industry and the multitude of choices that can be purchased for today's elk hunter, the options seem endless. In particular when you consider elk calls, new products appear each season. Everything from newly shaped mouth reeds, bugle tubes, push calls, and even sucker cow calls are now available in an attempt to help hunters sound more realistic to their quarry. Yet despite all the advancements, it seems so often during hunting season, when a bugle is heard, it's still easy to distinguish between a hunter's call and the real thing.

In the offseason it's not uncommon for me to be seen carrying a mouth reed in my truck. Attempting to sound more realistic as an elk caller is a never-ending process. Practicing a call in the cab of my rig might be likened to someone else's chance to sing in the shower. Having my own quiet studio as I'm driving an errand has been my time to practice calling without piercing my wife's ears around the house in the process. I may even be guilty of sending out the occasional cow chirp, chuckle, or a full-on elk bugle out the side window of my truck to some innocent bystanders along the road.

During one fall elk hunt in the middle of September, the calling action was picking up. I had been practicing my elk talk and was feeling confident we could lure in a bull. My brother Doug and

I had appeared to hit the rut at a perfect time, where we could pitch a bugle off the ridge top and receive a multitude of responses back. Our bugling practice was paying off!

On this particular morning, after casting out a bugle at first light, we heard an immediate response from across the nearest drainage. Unfortunately, the sound we received was the most whiny and strained bugle you could imagine. I immediately bemoaned the fact that another hunter had responded to our call as there was no way a real elk could sound that bad!

As we continued to make our way down the ridge, it was our goal to work away from the sound and try to locate an actual bull. However, as we descended further into the drainage, the hunter would not shut up. Poor pitched, weak bugling continued, responding even to our cow calls. To finally put an end to this exchange and continue with some "actual elk hunting," we decided to have some fun and call the hunter in. We figured once they saw we were not elk, they would finally cease their ear-piercing calling and move in the other direction.

It didn't take long before a few additional estrous whines pulled the hunter in on a string. However, as the sound coming through the trees finally revealed itself, our annoying hunter was sporting antler tips! This most unpleasant, poorly pitched, and whiny bugle was actually emerging from a 5x5 bull.

From that moment on, our vow moving forward was to never assume another bugle was a hunter. We committed to verify whether or not the sound we were hearing was the real thing before making an assumption and moving on. In the same way, often times there can be many different voices in our world pulling for our attention. With social media, news outlets, and acquaintances offering their opinions, it can be difficult at times to discern what and whom to listen to. However, Jesus reminded his followers that "I am the good shepherd" (Jn. 10:11) and my sheep need only to "listen to my voice" (Jn. 10:27).

Take time today to quiet yourself in the presence of your Creator and listen for His voice. His words are true and will not lead you astray. Be reminded that "For no matter how many promises

God has made, they are "Yes" in Christ" (2 Cor. 1:20). Get into His word and hear His words of truth. God is calling to us and wants to talk to us if we will only listen.

The Art of Waiting

*The Lord is good to those who wait for
him, to the soul who seeks him.*

(Lᴀᴍ. 3:25 ESV)

Wᴇ ʟɪᴠᴇ ɪɴ ᴀ society of instant gratification. As some psychologists would explain, it's our desire to gain immediate pleasure instead of waiting for a better return in the future. Why would we want to sit through commercials when we can use the DVR to skip to our favorite TV show? Why wait for food to slow roast in the oven when food cooked in a microwave is ready almost instantaneously? From instant access to news content or live social media posts on our phone, our brains have become accustomed to instant gratification.

As elk hunters we could occasionally use a heavy dose of patience. In this regard, I should have taken some of my own advice. While hunting some prime habitat in the eastern Oregon woods, it had been an exciting but unproductive week for our hunting party. We had all been continually into elk but couldn't fully close the deal. In my case, with the last day upon me before needing to exit early in order to make a mandatory work conference, I decided to hunt a promising bedding area I had located earlier in the day.

Walking stealthily with my face into the wind, GPS coordinates indicated the elk bedroom was a mere 100 yards away from my position. Traversing a well-used game trail, I took no more than a couple extra steps before branches began to break in the timber below me. With no time to think, I instinctively dropped five yards below the trail, tucking behind a small juniper.

In elk hunting, sometimes action happens so fast it's hard to process. In this instance, I barely had time to crouch down prior to antler tips emerging above the surrounding low-lying brush. A beautiful 6x6 bull had sauntered onto the game trail that just seconds prior had been my own path, and began walking straight in my direction. It was the moment of truth!

To this day, what happened next still feels like a slow-motion movie. As the bull's eyes were momentarily veiled by the juniper, I drew my bow. Focusing on my intended shooting lane all that emerged was a mass of brown fur a mere 5 yards away. As his front shoulder went past my sights I squeezed my release, and only milliseconds passed prior to my arrow hitting its mark, making a full pass through on this majestic animal. On the last day of the hunt with less than an hour of light remaining, I had scored the bull of a lifetime!

Under normal circumstances, it's customary to give an animal a minimum of several hours to expire. But given the shot placement and subsequent heavy blood trail, along with evening drawing near and my need to leave camp the next morning, I decided to push the envelope. My heart raced as the signs were clearly evident of a vital shot. It wasn't until I trailed the bull to the creek bottom that I heard commotion from the adjacent drainage face. Unbelievably, I watched in horror as my bull stood up from its death bed and began slowly walking away. As what would ultimately come to pass, despite hours of agonizing searching through the night and into the next morning, the blood trail had dried up and my bull of a lifetime was forever lost.

The art of waiting. Oh, how I wish I could go back and relive those moments, just simply giving him an hour or two before tracking the generous blood trail by flashlight, or waiting until morning to recover my bull. In our Christian walk it can be difficult to be patient and wait on the Lord. Yet waiting on God's answer, voice, and promise in prayer is an essential part of our walk with God.

The Bible offers several promises to the believers who wait and place their trust in the Lord. God wants to use waiting to bless our lives as the scripture says, "Yet the Lord longs to be gracious to you. . .Blessed are all who wait for him!" (Is. 30:18). There is also strength in waiting. "But those who wait for the Lord shall renew their strength. . ." (Is. 40:31a ESV) God also uses our patience and reliance on Him for our protection. "The Lord will fight for you; you need only to be still" (Ex. 14:14).

Take time today to quiet yourself amidst the busyness of life. Spend some alone time with your Creator, listening for His voice. God is faithful to speak to us through His Spirit, His written word and prayer. Take a moment today to simply quiet your heart and listen. Rushing foolishly into action can lead to disaster, but God is with those who patiently wait on Him.

Preseason Prep

A voice of one calling: "In the wilderness prepare the way for the Lord; make straight in the desert a highway for our God."
(Is. 40:3)

Sometimes the planning for a vacation is almost as much fun as the trip itself. I'm not sure if you have someone in your family who enjoys the prep work, but that is routinely a task I relish. Comparing flight itineraries, hotel options, driving routes, or sightseeing destinations—all the pre-trip research is a task that, to me, adds to the entire experience.

The same can be said around pre-season hunt planning. My wife might admit that once the fall elk hunting is complete, she witnesses discussions already being had for the following year. Next hunting season can't come soon enough!

Gaining advance knowledge about a particular hunting zone is an obvious benefit to any hunter. The more familiar and comfortable one can be prior to arriving at camp for the first day of the hunt only increases the odds of success. Not to mention, scouting trips are just flat out fun!

Typically, in either July or August, we combine our annual scouting excursion with various camp activities. Although we do spend a fair amount of energy hiking, glassing, and setting trail cameras, we also schedule time to simply unwind. Everything from campfires to ATV excursions, fishing, or long-distance rifle shooting, it's a great time to relax with family and friends. Of course, no camping trip would be complete without good eats. Let's just say I love my *Camp Chef* and we never return home hungry!

It has been estimated there are more than 300 prophecies about Jesus in the Old Testament. The prophets of old, like Isaiah, Elijah, and Ezekiel were proclaiming about the coming Messiah with prophecies concerning Jesus' birth, ministry, death, resurrection, and role in the future church. However, when Jesus arrived, not everyone was prepared to receive His message. Many were seeking an earthly king but Jesus had other plans. Jesus explained, "the Son of Man did not come to be served, but to serve, and to give his life as a ransom for many" (Mt. 20:28).

Just as the people of Israel were awaiting Jesus' arrival, so we today are anxiously anticipating His coming again. How are you preparing for Jesus' return? What type of fruit are you bearing? As Christ described in Matthew, "Not everyone who says to me, 'Lord, Lord,' will enter the kingdom of heaven, but only the one who does the will of my Father who is in heaven" (Mt. 7:21). May it not be said to us, "I never knew you" (Mt. 7:23a).

I encourage you to daily commit to following Christ. The Bible promises: "Come near to God and He will come near to you" (Jm. 4:8). Commit to doing some pre-season prep in your spiritual life, laying your foundation in Jesus. Our reward will be so much greater when one day we hear those words, "Well done, good and faithful servant! Come and share your master's happiness!" (Mt. 25:23).

Ready At Any Moment

For you know very well that the day of the
Lord will come like a thief in the night.

(1 Thess. 5:2)

I'm not sure about you but I love surprises. An unexpected gift, a spur of the moment trip away with my wife, or an unannounced visit by friends or family, surprises just add to the overall experience for me. However, I wouldn't apply this principle to hunting.

We talk a lot about being prepared for any situation in the woods because we never know when nature will throw us a curve ball. For instance, I remember one opening weekend during late August in the high Cascades. One hour we beheld nothing but blue skies while a few short hours later snow and hail were descending upon our camp. Or the time I was quietly side hilling along a timbered slope searching for elk when less than 40 yards below emerged a black bear sow and her cub. Although in both cases we escaped unharmed, encounters with unexpected predators, weather patterns, terrain features, or injuries can change a hunt plan in a hurry.

In an effort to be prepared for any circumstance, I take great care before ever leaving home to make a thorough list and accounting of necessary emergency gear. It's valuable to have equipment such as a satellite GPS communicator and first aid equipment in case of injury. Other essential items might include an emergency shelter, bear spray, topographical maps of my hunt unit, and a hunt plan left with someone at home so they know where you're going and when to expect you back. Yet all the planning in the world can't remedy laziness and stupidity.

It was a mid-September afternoon and solo hunting in Eastern Oregon had thus far been slow. Hot and dry weather were making for difficult stalking conditions. Beyond that, the forest was silent with nary a bugle to be heard, making locating any elk a challenge. After stacking days upon days of the same result, discouragement and apathy began to settle in.

Following another hard morning hunt with zero to show for my efforts, I decided to pack it in early. With my body fatigued and my mind craving the comforts of camp, I set a compass bearing for an early exit and began the 2-mile jaunt back to the trailhead. Letting discouragement get the best of me, I had strapped my archery gear to my backpack, removed my wrist strap release, and began hoofing it quickly across country as if hiking versus hunting. Despite walking through premium elk habitat as I moved along a well-used game trail, my mind had essentially given up on any prospects for the day. But as the saying goes, some of the best things in life appear when you least expect them.

After going day-after-day with no elk activity, you begin to believe the animals don't exist. But to my shock and horror, as I rounded a bend on the trail I was suddenly jolted back to reality as antler tips bobbed up and down moving straight in my direction. Caught empty handed, standing squarely in the middle of the game trail and with no cover in sight, my body froze. I watched in disbelief as a beautiful 5x5 bull sauntered right towards me. 50 yards, 40 yards, 30, 20, 10, the bull unbelievably walked to a mere three yards from where I stood. Locking eyes with this majestic creature and praying he wouldn't run me over, a momentary standoff ensued prior to the bull whirling and running gracefully over the hill. The bull I had been searching for all week was in arm's reach with no ability to respond. I was caught unprepared.

Of the 260 chapters in the New Testament, there are more than 300 references to the Lord's return—one mention out of every thirty verses! The world would like you to believe that a person can live for today and make peace with God before they die. Essentially, live however you want in this life and have time to reconcile your sin before meeting your creator. Yet Matthew 24:42 admonishes, "Therefore keep watch, because you do not know on what day your Lord will come."

None of us knows what the future holds. We are not even guaranteed tomorrow. As James 4:14 reminds, ". . .you do not even know what will happen tomorrow. What is your life? You are a mist that appears for a little while and then vanishes." God grants us every breath we take. We didn't bring ourselves into this world and no one knows the day or the hour of their departure. Our lives are in God's hands.

So, it begs the question, "Are you ready at any moment?" As 1 Thessalonians 5:2 warns, "for you know very well that the day of the Lord will come like a thief in the night." Matthew 24:27 goes on to describe, "For as lightning that comes from the east is visible even in the west, so will be the coming of the Son of Man." We need to be certain of our salvation today. Do not wait. Do not delay.

If you need to, stop where you are right now and commit your heart to God. Analogous to my bull encounter, don't be caught surprised or unaware in your own spiritual life. Make your peace with God today and be prepared for Christ's return.

Thermals Rule

The wind blows wherever it pleases. You hear its sound,
but you cannot tell where it comes from or where it
is going. So it is with everyone born of the Spirit.

(Jn. 3:8)

"Take this and rub it on your clothes," my dad would say as we came across a fresh elk bed. You're kidding me, right? You want your teenage son to do what? Pick up dirt and elk urine and rub that on my camo clothes?

When it came to elk hunting, you might say my dad was a little "old school." In his preparation for leaving camp, aside from his bow and arrows, his hunting supplies would often consist of merely a knife, compass, water, and an apple. Modern hunting items such as a GPS, headlamp, or range finder were either not yet invented or he refused to pack the extra weight.

However, when it came to wind thermals, although I never witnessed my dad utilize some of the modern conveniences of scent block spray or a wind check bottle, he was intuitively conscious of the importance of scent. His solution was if you can't look like an elk, you're going to smell like one!

Although my dad utilized a little more primitive means to try and block his human scent, I believe any elk hunter would agree the concept is universal. Wind is #1. In my experience, you can often get away with an elk hearing you, occasionally one seeing you, but it's impossible to beat their nose. If an elk smells you, the game is up. Thermals rule!

I couldn't count the number of times I have been moving in on a set-up, having the wind in my favor, only to have the thermals switch. You can have everything right but no control over the wind. We cannot see it but the thermals hold a powerful effect.

In many passages of Scripture, the Holy Spirit is described in a similar way. In explaining the workings of the Spirit, Jesus said to Nicodemus, "The wind blows wherever it pleases. You hear its sound, but cannot tell where it comes from or where it is going. So it is with everyone born of the Spirit." (John 3:8) Jesus promised His disciples that once He left, "You will receive power when the Holy Spirit comes on you" (Acts 1:8). As the early church was born on the day of Pentecost, "suddenly a sound like the blowing of a violent wind came from heaven" (Acts 2:2). This was the fulfillment of Jesus' promise to His disciples when He stated in John 14, "I will not leave you as orphans" (v.18), but instead, "I will ask the Father, and he will give you another advocate to help you and be with you forever" (v.16).

There is little in this life that you can classify as lasting forever. But this word offers me hope. So many things in our world are transient, here today and gone tomorrow. But we can rest in the knowledge that God has not left us alone. If we are in Christ, although we cannot see Him visually, His Spirit fills us and leads us.

Rest in the promise of the Holy Spirit being given to every believer. Allow the fresh wind of God's Spirit to blow through your soul today.

Can I Have a Do-Over?

I do not understand what I do. For what
I want to do I do not do. . .

(Rom. 7:15a)

It is difficult to think about all the years I have gone into hunting season full of hope and optimism only to end up eating "tag soup." Numerous conversations have been had on the drive home from elk camp about what we could have done differently. "If I hadn't taken that extra step I bet that bull wouldn't have busted." "If the wind didn't shift, I probably would have had a shot."

For any hunter who has stepped into the elk woods more than once, you likely understand my pain. Oftentimes you are offered only a few select opportunities at these elusive animals. We attempt to think in the moment of all the different variables that can affect our chances and up our odds of success—wind, yardage, obstacles, location, etc. So many factors and decisions are to be considered in the heat of the moment that, if not calculated correctly, can blow up a hunt. Sometimes you just want to say, "Can I have a do-over?"

During one memorable hunt, it was opening morning of deer and elk season in Oregon. I traveled pre-dawn to one of my favorite hunting spots that often held game. As the sun gradually peeked over the horizon, the dark outlines of several bodies began to materialize in the meadow below. An elk herd was feeding and moving my way.

Knowing the intricacies of the landscape well, I quickly positioned myself on the edge of the timber near a well-used game trail. As I continued to watch the elk feed in my direction, I knew that if I didn't spook them the herd would very likely get on the game trail I had selected and walk right past me. My mind was already celebrating an elk tag filled on opening morning!

Suddenly and without warning, the elk began to run. But to my surprise, they weren't running away but were heading straight towards me. Another hunter on the far side of the meadow had spooked the herd. Before I knew it, elk were streaming up the game trail so close I could literally reach out and touch them. One, two, three—cow after cow came flying by as I stood in a momentary trance. However, a huge antler rack snapped me back to reality as I caught the herd bull out of my periphery. A beautiful 6x6 was trailing his herd and would soon step within arm's reach of my present location.

Quickly knocking an arrow while my heart pounded out of my chest, I began timing in my mind when to draw. Given there was only a solitary tree between myself and the elk, I waited until the bull's eyes were momentarily hidden and I drew my bow. A slam-dunk shot from 5-yards. I couldn't miss!

What happened next is painful to recount. As I momentarily stood face-to-face with the herd bull, my arrow sat dangling harmlessly from its rest. When I had drawn my bow, the nock had pulled free from the arrow. An equipment malfunction had thwarted my golden opportunity.

In life, we can all agree that we make a multitude of mistakes. The apostle Paul understood the struggle between doing good and giving in to the sinful nature. He describes in Romans that "what I want to do I do not do, but what I hate I do" (Rom. 7:15b). He goes on to explain in verse 18b, "For I have the desire to do what is good, but I cannot carry it out." This struggle between good and evil is within all of us, because we were all born into sin. I can relate to Paul where he admits being "the worst of sinners" (I Tim. 1:16). The Bible also explains, "for all have sinned and fall short of the glory of God" (Rom. 3:23). But praise be to God that we are all afforded a "do-over."

God offers every person a second chance. Paul verbalized his deliverance as he went on to write, "Thanks be to God, who delivers me through Jesus Christ our Lord!" (Rom. 7:25). Jesus offers freedom to everyone; we simply need to believe. His promise is simple yet profound. "If you declare with your mouth 'Jesus is Lord' and believe in your heart that God raised him from the dead, you will be saved" (Rom. 10:9).

I pray today that you will seek after God. No mistake you have made is too big, no problem too great for our Savior. Ask for a "do-over." God is waiting.

Bibliography

Brainy Quote. "Epictetus Quotes." https://www.brainyquote.com/authors/epictetus-quotes.

Edison Innovation Foundation. "Importance of Thomas Edison Quotes." https://www.thomasedison.org/edison-quotes.

Frost, Robert, et al. *The Road Not Taken: A Selection of Robert Frost's Poems*. H. Holt and Co, 1991.

Goodreads. "Billy Graham Quotes." https://www.goodreads.com/quotes/306084-we-are-the-bibles-the-world-is-reading-we-are.

McDowell, Josh. *Evidence That Demands a Verdict*. Here's Life, 1989.

Minimalist Quotes. "Martin Luther Quotes." https://minimalistquotes.com/martin-luther-quote-109620.

Quotefancy. "Edward Way Quotes." https://quotefancy.com/quote/758509/Gerard-Way-One-day-your-life-will-flash-before-your-eyes-Make-sure-it-s-worth-watching.

Smithsonian National Air and Space Museum. "Multimedia Gallery." https://airandspace.si.edu/multimedia-gallery/failure-not-option-gene-kranz.

The Franklin Institute. "Benjamin Franklin's Famous Quotes." https://www.fi.edu/en/benjamin-franklin/famous-quotes.

Webster's Third New International Dictionary of the English Language. Merriam-Webster, 1993.

Wolfgang von Goethe, Johann. *Faust*. Bantam Classics, 2011.